State of the Union

THE NORTH'S CIVIL WAR
Paul A. Cimbala, Series Editor

1. Anita Palladino, ed., *Diary of a Yankee Engineer: The Civil War Diary of John Westervelt.*
2. Herman Belz, *Abraham Lincoln, Constitutionalism, and Equal Rights in the Civil War Era.*
3. Earl Hess, *Liberty, Virtue, and Progress: Northerners and Their War for the Union.* Second revised edition, with a new introduction by the author.
4. William L. Burton, *Melting Pot Soldiers: The Union's Ethnic Regiments.*
5. Hans L. Trefousse, *Carl Schurz: A Biography.*
6. Stephen W. Sears, ed., *Mr. Dunn Browne's Experiences in the Army: The Civil War Letters of Samuel W. Fiske.*
7. Jean H. Baker, *Affairs of Party: The Political Culture of Northern Democrats in the Mid-Nineteenth Century.*
8. Frank L. Klement, *The Limits of Dissent: Clement L. Vallandigham and the Civil War.* With a new introduction by Steven K. Rogstad.
9. Lawrence N. Powell, *New Masters: Northern Planters during the Civil War and Reconstruction.*
10. John Carpenter, *Sword and Olive Branch: Oliver Otis Howard.*
11. Thomas F. Schwartz, ed., *"For a Vast Future Also": Essays from the* Journal of the Abraham Lincoln Association.
12. Mark De Wolfe Howe, ed., *Touched with Fire: Civil War Letters and Diary of Oliver Wendell Holmes, Jr.* With a new introduction by David Burton.
13. Harold Adams Small, ed., *The Road to Richmond: The Civil War Memoirs of Major Abner R. Small of the Sixteenth Maine Volunteers.* With a new introduction by Earl J. Hess.
14. Eric A. Campbell, ed., *"A Grand Terrible Dramma": From Gettysburg to Petersburg: The Civil War Letters of Charles Wellington Reed.* Illustrated by Reed's Civil War Sketches.
15. Herbert Mitgang, ed., *Abraham Lincoln: A Press Portrait.*
16. Harold Holzer, ed., *Prang's Civil War Pictures: The Complete Battle Chromos of Louis Prang.*

State of the Union

NEW YORK AND THE CIVIL WAR

Edited with an Introduction by
HAROLD HOLZER

Foreword by
JEFF SHAARA

Published by
Fordham University Press
and New York State Archives Partnership Trust
2002

The North's Civil War, No. 17
ISSN 1089–8719

Library of Congress Cataloging-in-Publication Data

State of the Union : New York and the Civil War / edited with an
introduction by Harold Holzer ; foreword by Jeff Shaara.— 1st ed.
    p.   cm. — (The North's Civil War, ISSN 1089-8719 ; no. 17)
    Includes bibliographical references and index.
    ISBN 0-8232-2139-3 — ISBN 0-8232-2140-7 (pbk.)
    1. New York (State)—History—Civil War, 1861–1865—Congresses.
2. New York (State)—History—Civil War, 1861–1865—Social aspects—
Congresses.   3. United States—History—Civil War, 1861–1865—Social
aspects—Congresses.   4. Lincoln, Abraham, 1809–1865—Congresses.
I. Holzer, Harold.   II. New York State Archives Partnership Trust.
III. Series.
E523 .S73   2002
974.7′041—dc21   2001051057

Printed in the United States of America
01   02   03   04   05   5   4   3   2   1
First Edition

CONTENTS

FOREWORD

THROUGHOUT THE PAST SIX YEARS, I have traveled to nearly every state, doing book signings at the request of my publisher, speaking occasionally to groups of dedicated Civil War buffs, including Civil War Round Tables from San Diego to Spokane, Schenectady to Miami, Dallas to Fargo. And as my travels grew, the variety of the audiences grew as well. I found myself speaking to groups whose attendance had more to do with loyalty to their neighborhood bookstore than with any interest in the particular speaker addressing them. By the end of many an evening, however, these folks would ask many of the same impassioned questions that the die-hard Civil War buffs had addressed. Like so many historians and Civil War enthusiasts, I had assumed that we were a tightly knit bunch, with a passionate interest in the 1860s that most "other" people would find quaint or even a bit strange. But I received a pleasant surprise. I'm still not exactly sure what makes someone a "buff." But I have discovered that there are a great many people in this country who are searching for much more than what they found in their high school history textbook.

I have become accustomed to hearing the same question nearly everywhere I have spoken: *Why?* What is it about the American Civil War that generates such passion, enthusiasm, and a deep level of curiosity about the participants? Certainly throughout our history, there are events and crisis situations, monumental tales of heroism and struggle, whether one is looking back to 1776, 1941, 1968—or, in fact, today. But when we focus on the 1860s, there is something else at work, pulling us to a place beyond admiration of the good deed, the hero, the suffering of a nation and its people. I expected, of course, such passion for the subject in the South. Having grown up in Tallahassee, Florida, I was well aware that the "War of Northern Aggression" was continuing to rage. The wounds were still deep, and wide open. The loyalty and respect for men like Robert E. Lee were akin to worship. Thus, when I spoke to audiences in Virginia or Georgia or Tennessee, the response was predictable. I was gratified that appreciation of my stories was not constricted by notions of political correctness nor hampered by the controversies of modern "standards." In my work, I try to dig into the minds of characters such as Lee or Jackson, showing the reader *their* world as *they* saw it, without the crystal clarity of modern hindsight, without judgment or highhanded moralizing from our so superior vantage point in the twenty-first century. I was gratified that readers in the South seemed to appreciate my lack of bias, that I made the effort to bring them a story about one of their own without apology. What I did not expect was to hear from Southerners who not only enjoyed a visit with General Lee, but were intrigued as well with the character of Ulysses Grant, or the motivation that fueled the heroic drive in a man like Maine's Joshua Lawrence Chamberlain. My surprise continued: From readers far beyond Virginia, the letters and e-mails have come—some with emotion, some simply a thank-you—expressing appreciation for my efforts to tell an honest story of *all* these characters, regardless of which side they fought for, regardless of who "won."

I make no extraordinary claims as a revealer of truth or an uncoverer of hidden pasts. In following my father's daunting footsteps, to finish the Civil War story he began with *The Killer Angels*, my purpose was never more than to take myself, and then you, back to the time of these extraordinary events and, through the eyes of the characters, tell you their story as they might have told it themselves. Since I did not have my father's hand to guide me, I had to rely on his methods as I remembered them: walk the hallowed grounds, read the words, hear the voices of these men and women, find out from *them* how they experienced their world. Only by feeling that I *knew* them could I ever dare to speak for them. In some ways, going through this process changed my life. It certainly changed my view of history. But it was the impact of their voices on *you* that surprised me so.

I understand modern cynicism, that there is a great yawning abyss of respect for leadership in our time. It has become almost cliché that we are a nation struggling without our heroes. Ask any teenager whom he or she admires, and you will hear a litany of pop culture icons, musicians, athletes. But you are unlikely to hear the name of a politician or military commander. We middle-aged adults are old enough to remember John Kennedy or Dwight Eisenhower. Some of you have distinct recollections of Franklin D. Roosevelt, Harry Truman, Generals Patton or MacArthur. Whether or not we agreed with their politics or supported every decision they made, we all shared those innate feelings we have come to miss: Trust. Respect. Admiration.

I am rather amused when someone from another country laments that American history is not much of a history at all: too brief, compared, for example, to that of England. But dismissing America for its youth misses the point. History is not a measure of years, it is a measure of deeds. We are enormously blessed in this country to have a history that is explosively heroic, every generation responding to its own crisis with a forthright dignity, a display of honor and courage that defines, after all, what being an American was always supposed to mean.

In 1990, in the earliest days of the Gulf War, Saddam Hussein reportedly remarked that Americans had "no stomach for a fight." I would submit that Saddam had very little familiarity with Ethan Allen, Winfield Scott, Stonewall Jackson, Teddy Roosevelt, Omar Bradley—or Norman Schwarzkopf. But beyond our demonstrated passion for taking a fight to our enemies, we are forced to take pause when we dig into the 1860s. For this one terrible time, the enemy was ourselves. When we look back to find those shining moments when America vanquished her foes, we are caught in the uncomfortable glare of those four horrific years, held in the harsh light by more than curiosity. Our nation may have been born in 1776, but it was defined, and its preservation ensured, in 1865. That struggle was beyond anything we can comprehend today, and thus, the accomplishment of those people was beyond what many believe we could achieve today. And that is the appeal. We are a nation that has begun to look back to our own worst crisis, to explore and dig, inspired both by curiosity and need. It is why we so deeply appreciate the stories of those soldiers and statesmen, men or women who stood tall in one awful moment, those people who are not so very far removed from today. They are, in fact, *us*.

In this modern age of push-button war, Americans can lounge securely in their living rooms while their television follows a Cruise missile down a chimney in some far-removed place. We are certainly justified in feeling pride in our technology. But there is enormous danger in our ability to sanitize war, to observe that Cruise missile destroying a building without seeing who might have been inside. The same danger exists for the military commander, who can destroy his enemy from the safety of the far-distant aircraft carrier, or some technicians' perch in a satellite control room in Washington. If you do not see the face of your enemy, if you do not witness firsthand the horror of war, if the death and destruction is little more than a television show, then there is no motivation to make it end, or to prevent it from occurring again. As advanced as is our technology, ultimately, it is the document, or the photograph, that conveys the most powerful message.

Whether or not you admire the politics of Robert E. Lee, you must appreciate that this man faced his starving troops, realizing that the faith of his nation, the survival of his cause, was perched squarely on the backs of the men who called out to him with extraordinary affection wherever he went. If you believe that Ulysses Grant was a butcher, you must appreciate that this was a man who, above all else, understood the viciousness of war, that wars do not end unless the enemy is *defeated,* in all the ways that word is defined. Though the cost was horrific for both sides, Grant found a way to defeat the spirit and the will of Lee's army and bring to an end the most tragic chapter in our history.

In New York, we are blessed with people who have the passion and commitment to preserve and make available to all of us a wonderful store of information—the words, pictures and documents, the very details of who we are, and where we come from. To those Americans who understand the value of their legacy, there is no greater responsibility to ourselves and to our children than to keep alive the memories of our heroes. They *must* be remembered.

JEFF SHAARA
November 2000

PREFACE

THREE YEARS AGO, in celebration of the publication of the *Union Preserved: A Guide to the Civil War Records in the New York State Archives*, the New York State Archives, a program of the New York State Education Department, held a two-day symposium featuring research by leading scholars on New York's role in the Civil War. The symposium brought together a broad spectrum of attendees from the Lincoln Forum, Civil War re-enactors, Civil War Roundtable members, students, local historians, educators, and history enthusiasts. Among the attendees was Governor George Pataki, whose personal passion for history extends to an admiration for the work of Civil War historical novelist Jeff Shaara, the symposium's keynote speaker. All were drawn to the event by a rich and accessible program, examining not only New York's military role, but also the social, political, and internal economic contours of the conflict in New York. Many left the symposium feeling that they had attended a unique event, where New York State's pivotal role in the Civil War was truly examined and discussed for the first time.

As the most populous state at the time of the Civil War, New York was central to winning the war. The state provided not only the most men and materiel, but it was also the North's economic center as well as an important center of political and social activism. Inhabited by increasing numbers of immigrant groups, abolitionists, and an emerging free black community, New York's social and political environment was a microcosm of the larger social and political conflict being played out in the war. The symposium addressed these tensions by examining the role of women, blacks, Native Americans, and European immigrant groups in New York, particularly the various perspectives held by members of each group regarding the war effort. The symposium examined the difficulties Abraham Lincoln faced in keeping New York favorable to his policies. It revealed the tremendous sacrifice New York made in the military campaign, as well as the treatment of Confederate soldiers at New York's Elmira Prison

Camp. This publication, *The State of the Union,* is a compilation of the papers presented at the symposium.

The State of the Union is the second joint publication effort undertaken by the Archives Partnership Trust with Fordham University Press. The Partnership Trust is most pleased to continue working collaboratively with Fordham to bring attention to the New York State Archives and its efforts to advance new research using historical records in New York archives. New York State has more than 3,000 community historical societies and over 4,400 units of local government, as well as the State Archives in Albany, all of which hold tens of millions of historical records. For more than ten years, the State Archives has provided leadership statewide to ensure that these records, documenting the State's legacy, are preserved and made accessible for research, education, and lifelong-learning. The research presented at the symposium drew from these rich archival holdings and also revealed continued need to delve further into these extraordinary collections. The State Archives' Civil War holdings alone are the largest collection of Civil War archives among the states of the union, but are vastly untapped; as historian James M. McPherson has stated, they constitute "a gold mine."

This book would not have been possible without the commitment of renowned Civil War and Lincoln author Harold Holzer, who is also a member of the Archives Partnership Trust Board. Mr. Holzer took on the role of editor for this book, compiling and editing the various papers into a book manuscript, as well as handling many of the tiny details required to bring this project from concept to final published form. We are deeply indebted to Mr. Holzer for this exceptional work, as well as his continuing championing of the State Archives and the Partnership Trust.

The Partnership Trust and the State Archives also extends thanks to the wonderful symposium presenters, whose enthusiasm for this project continued long after the symposium ended. The synergy and sense of family that came from the symposium has created a lasting bond of collegiality and support.

Finally, this publication would not have been possible without the private support given the State Archives through the Partnership Trust. As a 501(c)(3) public benefit corporation created solely to support the State Archives, the Partnership Trust receives gifts from individuals, foundations, and corporations. This support was essential to producing the Civil War symposium and this new publication.

V. CHAPMAN-SMITH
New York State Archivist
Executive Officer, Archives Partnership Trust
www.nysarchives.org

INTRODUCTION AND ACKNOWLEDGMENTS

"This," declared Abraham Lincoln once civil war became inevitable in 1861, "is essentially a People's contest." The time had come, he urged loyal Americans, "to go forward without fear . . . to preserve the government, that it may be administered for all." No people responded to the President's call more quickly, more fearlessly, or more generously than did the citizens of New York State.[1]

Surviving enrollment records are imprecise because they include, but do not isolate, re-enlistments. But most experts agree that New York went on to supply more than 17 percent of all the troops who fought for the Union over the next four years—53,114 of whom sacrificed their lives—more by far than from any other state.[2] The Empire State would also contribute more funds than any other to the long, expensive war effort. And made-in-New York technology would help propel war into the modern age, as the first ironclad vessel took shape in a Brooklyn shipyard and fearsome advanced artillery was developed up the Hudson River at the foundries in Cold Spring.

As the war dragged on, the State made other, intangible contributions as well, leading the nation, for example, in publishing. New York-based suppliers of patriotic engravings and lithographs—from Currier & Ives and H. H. Lloyd of Manhattan to Cosack & Co. of Buffalo—supplied mass-produced portraits of military heroes and colorful scenes of battlefield triumphs for display in homes across the North, boosting morale. And Broadway portrait photographer Mathew Brady abandoned his plush studio and headed off to the battle zones along with his skilled camera operators to capture the grue-

---

[1] Roy P. Basler, editor-in-chief, *The Collected Works of Abraham Lincoln* 9 vols. (New Brunswick, NJ: Rutgers University Press, 1953–55), 4: 438, 440, 439.

[2] James M. McPherson, *For Cause and Comrades: Why Men Fought in the Civil War* (New York: Oxford University Press, 1997), 180.

some reality of the "grim-visaged war" for a horrified but fascinated public.[3]

The most important newspaper in the nation, the *New York Tribune*, operated profitably and influentially from its Manhattan headquarters, notwithstanding the fact that its editor, Horace Greeley, would famously urge young men to go west. The rival *New York Herald* sent no fewer than 63 correspondents to report on battles during the course of the war, keeping the city and the nation informed.[4] Yet another New York journal, the anti-war *World*, claimed the dubious distinction of becoming the only newspaper Abraham Lincoln ever ordered personally be shut down, for printing a forged presidential proclamation (the order was rescinded, and the paper reopened, three days later).[5]

No Civil War armies ever waged a formal battle in New York. But in July 1863, Union forces, some of whom were exhausted survivors of the recent combat at Gettysburg, were dispatched to put down the horrific Draft Riots that exploded through the streets of Manhattan. Meanwhile, in upstate Elmira, a Union military prison camp housed captured Confederate soldiers in conditions no less squalid than at the notorious Andersonville in Georgia. Yet this same state would generously host Sanitary Fairs to raise funds for wounded soldiers, float bonds to finance the war effort, and organize a new Workingwomen's Protective Association to assist "seamstresses, dressmakers, teachers and operatives in every branch of labor"[6] who yearned for opportunity and fair wages. Then as now, New York was a vast region of stark contrasts, impassioned loyalties, and enormous energy.

Although partisan politics continued throughout the war to divide the state—New York City remained strongly Democratic, while the counties north of Westchester stayed just as strongly Republican—homefront support for the war effort, casualties notwithstanding, generally held firm, manifested in both large and small ways, in pub-

[3] *Humphrey's Journal* for October 1861, quoted in Dorothy Meserve Kunhardt and Philip B. Kunhardt, Jr., *Mathew Brady and His World* (Alexandria, VA: Time-Life Books, 1977), 60.

[4] J. Cutler Andrews, *The North Reports the Civil War* (Pittsburgh, PA: University of Pittsburgh Press, 1985 edition of 1955 original), 20.

[5] Robert S. Harper, *Lincoln and the Press* (New York: McGraw-Hill, 1951), 289–99.

[6] Mary Elizabeth Massey, *Women in the Civil War* (orig. pub. in 1966 as *The Bonnet Brigades*, New York: Bison Books, 1994), 345.

lic and in private alike. Some citizens expressed their patriotic enthusiasm by attending mass rallies or, of course, enlisting. Others manifested their devotion to the Union by offering modest, handmade gifts to their heroes. "What *do* you think I received as a present yesterday?" a rather unappreciative General George B. McClellan wrote his wife in 1861. "Some poor woman away up in New York sent me a half dozen pair of woolen socks."[7] President Lincoln proved far more grateful when the New York Workingmen's Democratic Republican Association offered the President an honorary membership in their organization in 1864. Lincoln "gratefully accepted" the honor, thinking perhaps that this at last made him something of an honorary New Yorker in a city whose voters, he knew, had never supported him politically.[8] Turning serious in his letter of acceptance, he recalled the bloody legacy of the New York Draft Riots the year before, in which African Americans had been tortured and murdered by whites, and added this appeal for solidarity among people fighting to preserve freedom and opportunity: "The most notable feature of a disturbance in your city last summer, was the hanging of some working people by other working people. It should never be so. The strongest bond of human sympathy, outside of the family relation, should be one uniting all working people, of all nations, and tongues, and kindreds."[9]

As Lincoln and his contemporaries well knew, New York and its citizens of "all tongues and kindred" remained, throughout the Civil War, crucial to Union success. As he had vowed in Manhattan a few days before his 1861 inaugural: "There is nothing that can ever bring me willingly to consent to the destruction of this Union, under which not only the commercial city of New York, but the whole country has acquired its greatness." For the persistent and indispensable loyalty of New Yorkers, he had told well-wishers in Troy, he held "feelings of profound gratefulness."[10] Lincoln returned the favor in early 1864 by donating the handwritten copy of his preliminary Emancipation

---

[7] Herman Hattaway and Archer Jones, *How the North Won: A Military History of the Civil War* (Urbana, IL: University of Illinois Press, 1983); also quoted in George B. McClellan, *McClellan's Own Story* (New York: Charles L. Webster & Co., 1887), 13.

[8] *Collected Works of Lincoln*, 4: 232.

[9] *Collected Works of Lincoln*, 7: 259.

[10] Ibid., 4: 233, 227.

Proclamation to the Albany Army Relief Bazaar. There it was purchased for $1,000 by the noted abolitionist Gerrit Smith, who in turn
donated it back to another war charity organization, the United States
Sanitary Commission, from which the State of New York purchased
it in April 1865 for another $1,000. Today the document resides in
the New York State Museum—tangible evidence of Lincoln's respect
for and dependence on the Empire State.[11]

Yet gratitude and respect alone do not always stimulate history,
and despite New York's indisputable Civil War legacy, the literature
on the subject has remained surprisingly and painfully scant for generations. Save for the obligatory regimental histories, scholars have
understandably focused their attention on those states where armies
had met in battle. Aficionados can visit sites in Virginia, Pennsylvania,
and Maryland where battlefields have been lovingly preserved. In
New York, by contrast, the "colored orphan's asylum" that was
burned to the ground by rampaging rioters in 1863 long ago gave
way to commercial development on Fifth Avenue near the New York
Public Library. The persistent, irreversible disappearance of New
York's scarce but meaningful Civil War sites has made it easier for
twenty-first–century Americans to all but ignore the state that raised
so many of the soldiers, and provided so much of the wealth to support them.

The trend finally began reversing in 1999. That June, the New
York State Archives Partnership Trust, together with a national orga-
nization, The Lincoln Forum, and the Capital District Civil War
Round Table, jointly sponsored a well-attended landmark symposium
at the New York State Museum in Albany: *The Union Preserved: New
York and the Civil War.*

The gathering, and an accompanying exhibition of seldom-seen
state-owned artifacts and documents, was planned primarily to celebrate publication of a new book entitled *The Union Preserved: A
Guide to Civil War Records in the New York State Archives.* This
was the first guide ever produced to catalogue the astonishingly rich
collection of Civil War materials that had been religiously collected
and loyally preserved by New York State. But as scholar after scholar

---

[11] Ibid., 5: 433. Lincoln donated the handwritten copy of his final Proclamation to
a Chicago war bazaar. The document remained in Chicago, where it was destroyed
in the great fire.

took the podium in Albany not just to celebrate the publication but "to examine the state's unique role in fighting the war and transforming the nation," it became apparent that in their commentary lay the seeds of what surely merited yet another book.[12]

Happily, nearly all of the gifted historians and experts who delivered papers at that memorable symposium quickly agreed to adapt and expand their lectures for this new project. V. Chapman-Smith, the New York State Archivist who serves also as Executive Officer of the Archives Partnership Trust, and whose leadership made the first book and the resulting symposium possible in the first place, committed her office to a second volume. So did the State's Archives Partnership Trust Board, on which I have been privileged to serve since 1994. And so too did Saverio Procario, the director of Fordham University Press, which published the initial book and from the start expressed enthusiasm for this successor project.

If *The Union Preserved* was designed to provide the essential tools for understanding, and researching, New York's Civil War role—supplying the "raw materials for history," as historian William C. Davis aptly described the result—this new book was conceived to offer interpretive accompaniment to that essential treasury. Fortunately, the interpreters proved more than equal to the challenge.

Iver Bernstein of Washington University, whose classic 1989 study of the New York City Draft Riots remains the standard reference, not only re-visited the subject, but added insightful new analysis about the little-known draft riots that occurred almost concurrently upstate.

Independent Civil War scholar Lonnie Speer opened new windows onto conditions at the Union military prison in Elmira. And Laurence M. Hauptman of the State University of New York at New Paltz offered a probing look at conditions facing the Iroquois of New York State—an all-but-forgotten Civil War minority.

Lillian S. Williams of the State University of New York at Albany offered a thought-provoking examination of women and African Americans living through the crucible of New York's war and its impact on race and gender.

And Hans L. Trefousse of the City University of New York pre-

---

[12] Brochure for *The Union Preserved* symposium, June 11–12, Cultural Education Center, Empire State Plaza, Albany, New York.

sented an address on New York's role in the impeachment of Lincoln's White House successor, Andrew Johnson. Professor Trefousse's speech not surprisingly attracted national television broadcast on C-SPAN, for it was delivered as New York—and the rest of the nation—again found itself living through the nightmare of a presidential impeachment. Finally, this writer offered a glimpse into Abraham Lincoln's complicated relationship with New York, and New York's with him.

Perhaps the most spirited session of all was provided by two sober judges—Joseph W. Bellacosa, then serving on the New York State Court of Appeals, and Frank J. Williams, then a Justice of the Superior Court of Rhode Island—both not only respected jurists but accomplished Lincoln students. The two judges offered opposing views on the subject of Lincoln and civil liberties, enlivening one of the most provocative events of the symposium.

The conference was blessed, too, by the addition of expert commentary from scholars whose contributions could not be included on these pages: these came from Howard E. Mitchell, historical consultant and technical advisor for several films and television series on the Civil War; and historian DeAnne Blanton of Arlington, Virginia. And an emotional highlight was provided by novelist Jeff Shaara, who has won enormous popular and critical acclaim for his Civil War fiction. His keynote address enthralled a large audience that included the State's "first" Civil War enthusiast, Governor George E. Pataki. Mr. Shaara subsequently agreed to adapt his remarks into a preface for this volume.

To all of these participants the editor is deeply grateful. I must also acknowledge John Hanna, chairman of the Archives Partnership Trust Board, for his unwavering support and encouragement. Judy Hohmann and the rest of V. Chapman-Smith's team at the State Archives provided their usual, invaluable help, as did Anthony Chiffolo, managing editor at Fordham University Press, and Loomis Mayer, who guided this project through the production phases.

Finally, this book, like the first, owes a special debt to Daniel Lorello, associate archivist at the New York State Archives, who delivered a fine paper of his own at the Albany Symposium on the subject of Lockwood Doty, founder of the nineteenth-century New York Bureau of Military Statistics. More to the point, Lorello compiled all of the records that were published in our first volume, *The Union*

Preserved, and provided two excellent essays explaining their use and analyzing their meaning. It is no exaggeration to say that without the contributions of this modern-day "Lockwood Doty," neither that book, nor this one, would have been possible.

HAROLD HOLZER
Rye, New York
January 1, 2001

State of the Union

1

Housekeeping on Its Own Terms: Abraham Lincoln in New York

Harold Holzer

OF ALL THE MANY INVITATIONS that Abraham Lincoln ever received, one of the most irresistible came from his friends in the Empire State. Come to New York, their letter proposed, to the largest municipality in the largest state in the country, to address a friendly "meeting of citizens" at the town's biggest auditorium, in the Cooper Union. "Your compliance," promised his hosts, "will afford the highest gratification to the people of this city."[1] The crowd would surely be large and enthusiastic, the press coverage intense, the political advantage unlimited.

Yet Abraham Lincoln declined. He did not go to Cooper Union.

Those familiar with the story of Lincoln's landmark Cooper Union Address—the fabled speech that propelled the man from the West to fame in the East, and ultimately, to the presidency—will no doubt recognize that this saga seems at odds with history. But the story is actually true. Lincoln may have accepted an earlier invitation to speak at Cooper Union—actually, for the record, it was originally an invitation to speak at Plymouth Church in Brooklyn, but the event was moved across the river to Cooper Union in Manhattan when more tickets were sold than the church could hold—but he did in fact turn down the request that he return to the scene of that success only three years later.

The encore opportunity came in November 1863. Federal forces had won major victories at Gettysburg and Vicksburg the previous July, arguably turning the tide of the Civil War against the Confeder-

---

[1] George Opdyke, Joseph Sutherland, Benjamin F. Mannierre, Prosper M. Wetmore, and Spencer Kirby to Abraham Lincoln, November 38, 1863. Abraham Lincoln Papers, Library of Congress.

acy. Only a few days before the second Cooper Union invitation arrived, Lincoln had consecrated the Gettysburg triumph with the greatest speech of his career. At Gettysburg the war had been rededicated to "a new birth of freedom," but New York City remained haunted by the acrid memory of the racist draft riots that had swept through Manhattan that summer. Against this complex backdrop, the commander-in-chief had issued a call for new volunteers. This was the presidential action that triggered the presidential invitation. In response to Lincoln's call for troops, local supporters planned the pro-Union, pro-Lincoln rally at Cooper Union, and invited the President "to encourage by your voice the active efforts of the loyal men of this City in support of the Union cause." It seemed, to paraphrase Lincoln's remarks at Gettysburg, an "altogether fitting and proper" venue.[2]

It is unimaginable that a modern President would reject such a chance. Live coverage on CNN would be guaranteed. Soap operas would be interrupted in mid-scene to switch to the presidential appearance. And a hand-picked crowd would be on hand to cheer on cue. Even in Lincoln's era, a president was no less likely to be showered with attention and affection at such an event. "Nevertheless," Lincoln insisted in his reply, "the now early meeting of congress, together with a temporary illness"—he had come down with a mild but debilitating case of smallpox right after delivering his Gettysburg Address nine days earlier—"render my attendance impossible." He would do no more than send a letter to be read aloud at the meeting. That letter did reveal a Lincoln at the peak of his rhetorical power: "Honor to him," he declared, "who braves, for the common good, the storms of heaven and the storms of battle." The words suggest that the second Cooper Union address might have been even greater than the first.[3]

But Abraham Lincoln remained a virtual stranger to New York throughout his presidency. He did choose a leading New Yorker, former Senator and Governor William H. Seward, as his Secretary of State, and later selected a New York editor, Henry J. Raymond of *The New York Times,* to manage his 1864 re-election campaign. He

---

[2] Ibid.
[3] Roy P. Basler, editor-in-chief, *The Collected Works of Abraham Lincoln,* 9 vols., hereafter cited as *Collected Works of Lincoln* (New Brunswick, NJ: Rutgers University Press, 1953–55), 7: 32.

judiciously dispensed (and, when it suited him, withheld) patronage to New York and New Yorkers, and kept fully abreast of political developments in the state. He maintained cautious contact with *New York Tribune* editor Horace Greeley throughout the war, jousting with him publicly on Emancipation policy ("My paramount object in this struggle *is* to save the Union, and is not either to save or destroy slavery")[4] even after he had privately determined to issue a proclamation following the next Union battlefield victory.

Although he had made one of his most important pre-presidential appearances in New York at Cooper Union, during his White House years Lincoln stayed away from the nation's largest and most populous state. A public figure who eschewed presidential speechmaking generally (Gettysburg was a rare exception), he steadfastly resisted opportunity after opportunity to visit the nation's commercial capital to express himself publicly and personally on any subject. Lincoln's reluctance recalls a vastly different political culture, in which presidents seldom used the "bully pulpit" to win the support of the American people. Such appeals were, by tradition, made in state papers or through surrogates and sympathetic journalists. As important as New York remained to Lincoln and the war effort, it must be said that Lincoln never regarded his personal appearance in New York as crucial to his political success there.

Surely, it was not for lack of confidence. As Horace Greeley's newspaper recalled of Lincoln's Cooper Union speech back in February 1860: "No man ever before made such an impression on his first appeal to a New York audience."[5] *The New York Tribune* reprinted the speech in full, and promptly published a pamphlet version as well.

To make certain that "such an impression" was distributed even further, the city's leading photographer, Mathew Brady, arranged to take Lincoln's picture while he was in the city. In posing him at his studio, Brady moreover had the good sense to tug up Lincoln's shirt collar to cover his long, scrawny neck before making the photograph. The flattering likeness that resulted was so widely reproduced during the presidential campaign that Brady, perhaps without too much bravado, claimed it "was the means of his election."[6]

---

[4] Ibid., 5: 388.

[5] *New York Tribune*, February 28, 1860, quoted in Mario M. Cuomo and Harold Holzer, eds., *Lincoln on Democracy* (New York: HarperCollins, 1990), 164.

[6] Francis B. Carpenter, *Six Months at the White House: The Story of a Picture* (New York: Hurd & Houghton, 1866), 47.

Historians have consistently echoed Greeley's assessment of Lincoln's Cooper Union appearance. Most recently, historian David Herbert Donald called it both a "success" and "a superb political move." But votes speak louder than words. The approbation of pro-Republican publishers like Greeley, and self-aggrandizing image-makers like Brady, can be deceptive.[7]

On election day, 1860, less than nine months after he allegedly won the hearts of New York City at Cooper Union, Lincoln decisively lost the vote at the local polls in the contest for the presidency. Stephen A. Douglas beat him by 24,000 votes in Manhattan, by 5,000 in Brooklyn, and by 2,500 in Westchester. Lincoln fared much better upstate, where, ironically, he had never spoken and rarely visited. (Even when he first saw, and deeply felt, what he called the "mysterious power" of Niagara Falls, the interesting little essay that he wrote about the tourist mecca remained unpublished.) Like the nation itself, pre-war New York State was separated along rigid north-south borders that divided politics as well as geography. Our own "Mason-Dixon" line stretched across what is now Route 287 on the latitude of Tarrytown. South of that border, voters were staunchly Democratic, and not terribly sympathetic to African Americans. North, the sentiments were Republican, and perhaps a bit less racist than in the villages and towns below. On election day, 1860, only the overwhelming support of upstate precincts, where Lincoln had never delivered a speech, offset his disastrous showing downstate, to give him a 50,000-vote overall plurality that year statewide.[8]

Where New York State was concerned that pivotal year, the fact is that Abraham Lincoln did best where he was seen least. Under the circumstances, his reluctance to return should perhaps strike modern readers as unsurprising: the major media was concentrated downstate, but so were Lincoln's sharpest critics, and his weakest public support. As President, the greatest figure of the Civil War never made a public appearance in the largest state of his fragile Union.

In a way, Lincoln did "appear" in New York during the 1860 presi-

---

[7] David Herbert Donald, *Lincoln* (New York: Simon & Schuster, 1996), 240–41.

[8] *New York Tribune Almanac for the Years 1838 to 1864, Inclusive . . .* (New York: The New York Tribune, 1868), 41; *Collected Works* II: 10; for the statewide vote see Stefan Lorant, *The Glorious Burden: The History of the Presidency and Presidential Elections from George Washington to James Earl Carter, Jr.,* rev. ed. (Lenox, Mass.: Author's Edition, Inc., 1976), 1066.

dential campaign, but not in person. Engravings and lithographs based on Brady's Cooper Union photo were widely circulated instead. These images not only helped introduce Lincoln to Eastern Republican voters, they influenced one admirer to devise a plan to make the rapidly improving, but still frontier-inspired Lincoln image a bit more dignified. A little girl from Westfield, a village nestled along the state's Southern Tier in Chautauqua County, saw a Brady adaptation that her father brought home from a local fair. She liked Lincoln, but worried that the engraved print made him look too "thin." She had four brothers, and while "part of them will vote for you any way," she wrote in a charming personal letter to the candidate, "if you will let your whiskers grow I will try and get the rest of them to vote for you[.] You would look a great deal better. . . . All the ladies like whiskers and they would tease their husband's [*sic*] to vote for you and then you would be President."[9]

This was one New Yorker's invitation that Lincoln *did* accept, even though he first wrote little Grace Bedell a now-famous letter to the contrary. "As to the whiskers," he asked her, "never having worn any, do you not think people would call it a piece of silly affect[at]ion if I were to begin it now?" But within a month, the silly piece of affectation was not only sprouting from his face, but effectively changing his image from that of the western railsplitter who symbolized the limitless opportunities of the American dream (the print portrait Grace Bedell saw actually boasted a rail-fence border motif that so suggested) to that of a wise, bearded statesman equal to the secession crisis that awaited him in Washington.[10]

Historians have occasionally argued since then that Lincoln received so many other suggestions that he grow a beard that it is folly to credit one eleven-year-old New Yorker with influencing his decision. Lincoln himself would certainly have disagreed. When the train carrying him to Washington for his inauguration stopped in Grace Bedell's Westfield home town on February 16, 1861, Lincoln devoted what turned out to be his very first speech in New York State as

---

[9] Grace Bedell to Abraham Lincoln, October 15, 1860. Abraham Lincoln Papers, Library of Congress.

[10] *Collected Works of Lincoln*, 4: 129; the engraved campaign banner that Grace Bedell saw in 1860 is reproduced in Harold Holzer, Gabor S. Boritt, and Mark E. Neely, Jr., *The Lincoln Image: Abraham Lincoln and the Popular Print* (New York: Scribner's, 1984), 72.

president-elect to acknowledge her. Emerging from his train, he told the assembled crowd: "Some three months ago, I received a letter from a young lady here; it was a very pretty letter, and she advised me to let my whiskers grow, as it would improve my personal appearance; acting partly upon her suggestion, I have done so; and now, if she is here, I would like to see her."

And then, as a journalist on the scene reported: "A small boy, mounted on a post, with his mouth and eyes both wide open, cried out, 'there she is, Mr. Lincoln,' pointing to a beautiful girl with black eyes, who was blushing all over her fair face. The President left the car, and the crowd making way for him, he reached her, and gave her several hearty kisses, and amid the yells of delight from the excited crowd, he bade her good-bye. . . ."[11]

It was an auspicious, heartwarming upstate New York debut. Lincoln might have done well to harness the sympathy it generated by devoting the remaining speaking opportunities on his inaugural journey to more substantive reassurances to worried Northerners. But he failed to do so. In nearby Dunkirk, Lincoln did little more than feebly protest against all the demands upon him for further remarks: "Were I to stop and make a speech at every station, I would not reach Washington until after the inauguration." And in Buffalo, he called for public "composure," declaring that until he got "all the light I can," he would remain silent on major issues in order to avoid disappointing "the reasonable expectations of those who have confided to me their votes."[12]

Moving east to Batavia, he merely joked that he did not want to develop a reputation as "a talker;" at Rochester he protested, "I have not the strength" for speeches or interviews; in Clyde he said he "had no speech to make, and no time to make it in;" at Syracuse, he said he meant no "discourtesy" but was "unwilling" to ascend the speaker's platform erected in his honor; at Utica, he told the ladies gathered on one side of his railroad car that he had no time "to make remarks of any length," and then haltingly told the gentlemen massed on the other, "I can't . . . say here, exactly what I did on the other side, as there are no ladies on this side." Moving east, through Little Falls, Fonda, and Schenectady, his impromptu remarks, never Lincoln's

---

[11] *Collected Works of Lincoln,* 4: 219.
[12] Ibid., 220–21.

strong point, were hardly more inspired. The *Schenectady Evening Star* was probably being generous when it reported that "we were only able to obtain a few disjointed sentences" from the President-elect.[13]

Then he headed for Albany. In the "confusion, hurry, disorder, mud, riot and discomfort" reigning at the railroad station that day, excitement built to a fever pitch when the inaugural special steamed into sight. But when President-elect Abraham Lincoln finally emerged onto the platform in the capital of New York State, the crowd was at first too stunned to applaud. As a journalist on the scene explained, "standing uncovered . . . the President [*sic*] was barely recognized by the crowd, and anxiety to see him and to be certain that they saw the right man overcame any disposition to cheer." Ironically, those widely-circulated engravings and lithographs of the clean-shaven candidate may have proven a bit *too* effective. As the eyewitness correspondent pointed out: "Lincoln, tired, sunburned, adorned with huge whiskers, looked so unlike the hale, smooth shaven, red-cheeked individual who is represented upon the popular prints and is dubbed the 'rail splitter'; that it is no wonder that the people did not recognize him. . . ."[14]

But Lincoln wisely recognized New York. As he acknowledged in the capital, "the great Empire State at this time contains a greater population than did the United States of America at the time she achieved her national independence." He did not mention that it also contained similar geographic divisions. Perhaps he did not have to do so. Lincoln did express particular gratitude that his reception here had been proffered "without distinction to party," but out of a common desire "to perpetuate our institutions, and to hand them down to succeeding generations"—a clever reminder that he intended to be President of all Americans, notwithstanding the opposition of more than 60% of American voters nationwide at the polls the previous November. Yet he remained vexingly unwilling to reveal specifically how he proposed dealing with the seceded states once he took the oath of office less than two weeks later. Critics, and even some supporters, fretted that he was wasting an unprecedented chance to solidify support.[15]

---

[13] Ibid., 221–24.

[14] Harold G. Villard and Oswald Garrison Villard, *Lincoln on the Eve of '61: A Journalist's Story by Henry Villard* (New York: Alfred A. Knopf, 1941), 92–93.

[15] Ibid., 224–26.

Lincoln nonetheless maintained official silence the following day, as he headed south through Troy, Hudson, Poughkeepsie, Fishkill, and Peekskill toward New York City. There, the Cooper Union experience notwithstanding, Lincoln was greeted coldly by a "crowd not as large as usual," and apparently disinclined to proffer what sympathetic, on-the-scene observer Walt Whitman called "the glad exulting thunder-shouts of countless unloos'd throats of men." Whitman was relieved that no "outbreak or insult" had occurred, for as he put it, Lincoln "possess'd no personal popularity in New York and not much political." But to one who had witnessed "wild, tumultuous hurrahs—the deafening tumults of welcome, and the thunder-shouts of pack'd myriads along the whole of Broadway" to welcome lesser luminaries, the scene was, he confided, "almost comical."[16]

Matters in New York were perhaps worse than the chilly welcome indicated. Lincoln was surely not exaggerating when he called his New York welcoming committee "a people who do not by a majority agree with me in political sentiments." Publicly, Lincoln told Mayor Fernando Wood at City Hall: "There is nothing that can ever bring me willingly to consent to the destruction of the Union, under which not only the commercial city of New York, but the whole country has acquired its greatness." Privately—indeed, secretly—Wood's response was to hatch a plan to have the metropolis secede from the Union and establish itself as an international port. But when he learned of the Mayor's outrageous scheme, Lincoln merely drawled: "I reckon that it will be some time before the front door sets up housekeeping on its own terms." That time never came.[17]

New York City remained part of New York State, and New York State went on to contribute more men and materiel to the Union cause than any other. It would be wrong to suggest that just because many New Yorkers failed to appreciate Lincoln that Lincoln failed to appreciate New York. Even though he never fully embraced the state, he did rely upon it: for financial support for the war effort, for troops, and, as it turned out, for new technology as well.

---

[16] Earl Schenck Miers, ed., *Lincoln Day By Day: A Chronology, 1809–1865,* 3 vols. (Washington: Lincoln Sesquicentennial Commission, 1960), 3: 18; Andrew A. Freeman, *Abraham Lincoln Goes to New York* (New York: Coward-McCann, 1960), 108.

[17] Iver Bernstein, *The New York City Draft Riots: Their Significance for American Society and Politics in the Age of the Civil War* (New York: Oxford University Press, 1990), 143; *Collected Works of Abraham Lincoln,* 4: 232–33.

In New York State, it might be said, Lincoln first came dramatically face to face with the choice between the old and the new rules of war. In June 1862, the President came up from Washington for a visit to the Military Academy at West Point. There he talked strategy with his former general-in-chief, the aged Mexican War hero Winfield Scott. Although there is no record of their conversation, one can almost hear "Old Fuss and Feathers" reminding Lincoln of his vast experience in every American conflict since the War of 1812, and expounding on the rules of classic combat. But on that same trip, Lincoln also visited Robert Parrott's high-tech munitions foundry in nearby Cold Spring, a blazing furnace of mass-production, and then observed Parrott's new, rifled cannon hurling shells with deadly precision across the Hudson River, exploding onto targets painted on the cliffs on the opposite shore. Lincoln could not have departed the West Point area without the conviction that sophisticated, accurate, relentless modern weaponry would yet become the key to Union victory. By the end of the war, Parrott's West Point foundry would manufacture more than 1,700 guns and some three million projectiles.[18]

Perhaps the de-personalization of war epitomized by Parrott's long-distance weaponry encouraged Lincoln to distance himself further from the politically troublesome state where it was perfected. Perhaps travel of any kind became increasingly difficult for the beleaguered president. For whatever reasons, when draft riots convulsed New York City in July 1863, Lincoln received detailed reports of the violence and mayhem—one of them 22 pages long from Governor Horatio G. Seymour—but made no attempt to visit the city to help restore calm, or to console loyal New Yorkers once the disturbances had ended, even though he believed at one point that his own college-student son was visiting the city at the time and likely worried that he might be in personal danger.[19]

By contrast, only three months earlier, Lincoln's Confederate counterpart, Jefferson Davis, had made a heroic personal appearance

---

[18] Miers, *Lincoln Day by Day*, 3: 123; Patricia L. Faust, *Historical Times Illustrated Encyclopedia of the Civil War* (New York: Harper & Row, 1986), 816.

[19] See Seymour to Lincoln, July 24, August 1, August 3, 1863, Abraham Lincoln Papers, Library of Congress. See also John Jay to Lincoln, July 13, 1863, first informing him of the riots. Lincoln wrote the following day to his son, Robert, whom he believed to be staying at the Fifth Avenue Hotel in New York City: "Why do I hear no more of you?" See *Collected Works of Lincoln*, 6: 327.

at the site of the Richmond bread riots to plead for order. True, the Confederate disturbance occurred virtually in Davis's own back-yard—he could probably hear the shouting from his mansion, only a few blocks away. And true, the rioters in Richmond were all female, posing much less danger than marauding male New Yorkers bent on lynching and mutilating African Americans. But to his credit, Davis rushed to the scene, climbed atop an overturned wagon, and de-manded that the protesters disperse. By contrast, the New York City draft riots, to that point the most significant civil disorder in the en-tire history of the nation save for the Civil War itself, did not seem urgent enough for the President of the United States to impose on the confused scene what he had once described in Albany as "the representative of the majesty of this great nation"—that is, the Presi-dent himself. Lincoln sent troops. But he did not "mount the wagon" as Davis had done in Richmond.[20]

In fact, Lincoln never ventured to New York again. A proposal that he attend a celebration of the Henry Clay Club on Broadway on February 17, 1864, was ignored. So were two complimentary tickets accompanying an invitation to a "Monster Festival and Concert" of the Musical Mutual Protection Union of New York that September. And when, earlier that season, the President was invited to visit Sara-toga Springs, he replied by summoning another guest of the spa, Governor Edwin D. Morgan, to come visit him in Washington in-stead.[21]

And yet Lincoln surely understood the difficulty he faced in win-ning New York's crucial electoral votes in the November presidential election. He had even secured the services of Henry Raymond, editor of *The New York Times,* to serve as chairman of the Republican Na-tional Committee. Raymond, who raised a fortune for the fall cam-paign, remained convinced that Lincoln would lose the election, and did a great deal to help him win it.

Lincoln's relationship with the pro-Democratic *New York World*

---

[20] William C. Davis, *Jefferson Davis: The Man and His Hour* (New York: Harper-Collins, 1991), 497; *Collected Works of Lincoln,* 4: 226.

[21] Thomas E. Gildersleeve to Abraham Lincoln, February 9, 1864; John P. Cooke and others to Abraham Lincoln, September 5, 1864; and W. H. Deland & Co. to Abraham Lincoln, July 29, 1864, all in the Abraham Lincoln Papers, Library of Congress. Lincoln's wire to Governor Morgan is in *Collected Works of Lincoln,* 7: 474.

was rather different. When in 1863 the *World* brazenly published a forged Presidential proclamation calling for 400,000 new troops, in an apparent effort to inflate gold prices, Lincoln signed an order closing the paper down. It marked the only time in the war that he used his war powers to limit freedom of the press. Although the *World* was allowed to re-open a few days later, its editors resumed their relentless opposition to the Administration, and in particular directed their attention to ousting Lincoln from the White House in the election of 1864.[22]

No president had run successfully for a second term since Andrew Jackson, and unlike Lincoln, Jackson had not faced an electorate battered by the casualties and financial cost of a three-year-old rebellion that they had once been led to believe would be suppressed in three weeks. If war was not enough to turn the voters against Lincoln, some New Yorkers focused on another issue that was potentially even more incendiary: emancipation. The fragility of Lincoln's support was evident as early as August, when a local man named George Chopat wrote to the President to propose organizing "a Club to support your re-election . . . situated in a District (18th Ward) hitherto unapproachable by any but the rankest anti-administration kind." Chopat promised nothing less than "the planting of a *Union Flag* in the midst of Irish-American Copperheadism." But he would do so only on one condition: that Lincoln offer to re-admit the rebel states with the right to own slaves there intact. Lincoln had no intention of reversing the Emancipation Proclamation; Chopat's letter went unanswered and so, presumably, died his offer of founding a Lincoln club in the unfriendly confines of Democratic Manhattan.[23]

The *New York World* waged a more overt campaign to derail the President's re-election. The paper not only issued a series of editorials assailing Lincoln's candidacy, but oversaw the production and distribution of a series of hostile, racist cartoons that suggested that Lincoln was plotting to integrate Northern society if he were returned to the White House. One such lampoon showed him presiding over a cotillion at which white people worked as servants and black people frolicked as guests; another portrayed Lincoln in black-

---

[22] Robert S. Harper, *Lincoln and the Press* (New York: McGraw-Hill, 1951), 289–93, 296–99.

[23] George Chopat to Lincoln, August 24, 1864, Abraham Lincoln Papers, Library of Congress.

face, playing the title role of the Moor in Shakespeare's *Othello*. All of the cartoons were designed to inflame racial prejudice in a City still reeling from the after-shock of the 1863 Draft Riots. In 1864, the threat of so-called racial "amalgamation" still sent tremors of fear into frightened white communities.[24]

At one point, the *World* also masterminded a dirty-trick campaign against Lincoln. How close it came to succeeding we do not know. The newspaper issued a bizarre book produced by David Goodman Croly and George Wakeman, entitled *Miscegenation: the Theory of the Blending of the Races*. It not only introduced "miscegenation" into the national vocabulary as the new word for race-mixing, but suggested the advantage of such a system as a "positive gain" for the Irish. The authors, of course, believed nothing of the kind; their straight-faced endorsement of racial integration was designed to arouse fear, not hope, among white voters.[25]

The publishers proceeded to send Lincoln a copy of the tract and invited his endorsement, no doubt hoping that he would praise it with words that could be used by his enemies to confirm the President's supposedly radical liberalism on issues of race. Instead, Lincoln turned the tables on the hoaxters by leaking their scheme to the press himself. "This dodge will hardly succeed," the *London Morning Herald* reported, "for Mr. Lincoln is shrewd enough to say nothing on this unsavory subject." Instead, Lincoln wisely filed away his copy of this New York-produced book. It was not discovered until his official papers were opened to the public at the Library of Congress in 1947.[26]

Notwithstanding the challenges facing the Lincoln campaign in 1864, the candidate stayed away. An August 1864 invitation by the Union League to address a rally in Buffalo was first ignored, then lost, and finally rejected. "I believe it is not customary for one holding the office, and being a candidate for re-election," to campaign in

---

[24] For examples of these cartoons, see Mark E. Neely, Jr. and Harold Holzer, *The Union Image: Popular Prints of the Civil War North* (Chapel Hill: University of North Carolina Press, 2000), 151–59.

[25] See *Miscegenation: The Theory of the Blending of the Races, Applied to the American White Man and Negro* (New York: Croly and Wakeman, 1864). Lincoln's copy is in the Library of Congress. See also, Sidney Kaplan, "The Miscegenation Issue in the Election of 1864," *Journal of Negro History*, 34 (July 1949), 324.

[26] See Harold Holzer, ed., *The Lincoln Mailbag: America Writes to the President, 1861–1865* (Carbondale, IL: Southern Illinois University Press, 1998), 176–78.

person, Lincoln explained. Instead, as was his custom, he produced a superb letter and asked that it be read aloud at the meeting, declaring: "No man desires peace more ardently than I. Still, I am yet unprepared to give up the Union for a peace, which, so achieved, could not be of much duration." Abandon Emancipation, he insisted, "and the Union goes with it." "It can not be; and it ought not to be."[27]

More difficult to comprehend was Lincoln's indifferent reaction to an almost irresistible invitation to return to Manhattan to speak at a non-political "Mass Assemblage" in Union Square in June 1864, in honor of General Grant. Lincoln would only explain: "It is impossible for me to attend."[28]

Here was another politically promising chance to be seen by the public in an evocatively symbolic setting (the scene of the first pro-Union rallies of April 1861), in a vital state that the newly re-nominated President needed desperately to win in order to secure re-election that November. But once again, it was an opportunity lost. Lincoln would go on to win New York State on election day, but just barely. In fact, his majority in the state declined from 53.7% in 1860 to just 50.4% in 1864, and his chances of victory here remained very much in question until the final votes were counted on election night. Ultimately, the state did go Republican, electing a pro-Lincoln governor (who received a greater majority than did the man at the top of the ticket), along with a Republican legislature and an overwhelmingly Republican Congressional delegation. Perhaps Lincoln believed that a return visit to Cooper Union would not have improved his chances.[29]

At least it was a New Yorker who wrote to Lincoln to offer an amateurish but heartfelt poetic tribute in celebratory anticipation a day before his re-election:

> Ho, Freemen to the rescue! Our Lincoln lead the van,
> A patriot true and statesman—a tried and honest man!
> When treacherous sands and ice-bergs the Ship of State surround,
> *His* trumpet from the quarter-deck gives no uncertain sound.[30]

---

[27] *Collected Works of Lincoln*, 8: 1–2.

[28] F. A. Conkling, Charles H. Marshall and others to Abraham Lincoln, May 31, 1864, Abraham Lincoln Papers, Library of Congress; *Collected Works of Lincoln*, 7: 374.

[29] Lorant, *The Glorious Burden*, 1066–67.

[30] H. O. Newman to Lincoln, November 7, 1864, Abraham Lincoln Papers, Library of Congress.

Such sentiments suggest that Lincoln may have underestimated the growing affection and loyalty of New York and New Yorkers. A month before delivering his Gettysburg Address, he was so reminded by a poignant letter signed by 118 self-described "poor boys" from a charity school called the House of Industry in the notorious Five Points slum of Manhattan. During his Cooper Union trip to New York three years earlier, Lincoln had paid a Sabbath visit to the orphanage, where he told the downtrodden children, as they now gratefully reminded him, that "the way was open to every boy present, if honest, industrious, and perserv[er]ing, to the attainment of a high position." Now that the unknown western stranger of 1860 had gone on to prove instrumental "in liberating a race, and in leading your countrymen through present troubles," the orphans wanted to acknowledge that Lincoln's "own life history illustrates the truth of the words you then addressed to us." They closed by asking God to "ever own and bless you and yours."[31]

Then, just two months before his death, he received a deeply moving tribute to "Our Beloved and Honored President" from an admirer in Troy. Thrilled that Lincoln would be *our President Again*," Sarah T. Barnes wrote:

> I do so thank God for it all; and for making you our President the second time. God has helped you or you never could have lived through what you have; of course, He will stand by, and uphold you; and be assured there are thousands of warm true hearts all over this noble country, who love and honor you, and pray for you, too, every day. Ah! Mr. Lincoln the nation's hopes are centered in you; the national heart beats loyally for you. God bless you fully and richly![32]

It was one of the last, and certainly one of the most enthusiastic, such tributes that Lincoln ever received. But when he was assassinated in April 1865, New York State again paid tribute at a series of emotional funerals that re-traced in reverse, and with far more emotion, the route of his awkward, uninspiring inaugural journey four years earlier.

In some ways, New York City had learned little from the lessons

---

[31] Patrick McCarty and others to Lincoln, October 16, 1863, Abraham Lincoln Papers, Library of Congress.

[32] Sarah T. Barnes to Lincoln, February 7, 1865, Abraham Lincoln Papers, Library of Congress.

of war and Lincoln's leadership. When a delegation of African Americans proposed marching in the Manhattan funeral procession, the Common Council voted to bar them. Only when the local Union League intervened did Secretary of War Edwin M. Stanton urge that the black New Yorkers be permitted to march. Even so, they were relegated to last place at the tail end of the long line of marchers paying tribute that day to the fallen President.[33]

The next morning, the Lincoln funeral train headed slowly north along the Hudson before turning west toward the Great Lakes, passing beneath floral arches erected in tribute over the tracks at towns all along the route. Thousands of mourners lined the route to view the train as it rolled by, waving handkerchiefs and sobbing openly. Emotions ran so high in Buffalo that the City prematurely staged a memorial service that drew huge throngs, only to learn that Lincoln's remains would be brought there a few days later. A second funeral was hastily arranged, and 100,000 people came back a second time to mourn.[34]

In Poughkeepsie, thousands packed the small hilltop depot where the train paused as Matthew Vassar, founder of the local college, carried into the car bearing the coffin a bouquet of magnolias he had cut from his own tree. It proved one of the most touching moments among the many tributes paid to the martyred Lincoln.

Of course, events somehow always unfold uniquely in the state capital. There, the city was getting ready to welcome, of all things, a traveling menagerie—a street parade featuring giraffes, bears, tigers, leopards, lions, deer, and for good measure, an ostrich—when the event was abruptly postponed and a Lincoln funeral procession substituted. That day, bells tolled throughout Albany and the streets filled with mourners as Lincoln's body was transported through the streets. But the very next day, once the train had moved on, the lions, tigers, and bears arrived to take the same route, merely one day later than scheduled. Welcoming the delayed menagerie, Albany returned to normal.[35]

---

[33] Dorothy Meserve Kunhardt and Philip B. Kunhardt, Jr., *Twenty Days*. . . . (New York: Harper & Row, 1965), 154; Edwin G. Burrows and Mike Wallace, *Gotham: A History of New York City to 1898* (New York: Oxford University Press, 1999), 904–905.

[34] Kunhardt and Kunhardt, *Twenty Days*, 218.

[35] Ibid., 172–73.

One almost senses that had Lincoln been sent these final invitations, he would probably have declined them, too. He never overcame his Whiggish resistance to public appearances and public speaking after his election as President. He made precious few presidential addresses. And he was never prepared to make New York an exception to his rule of attending to the people's business at the White House.

But the *New York Herald* viewed matters differently. Comparing his frigid welcome back in 1861—when Lincoln was both "scoffed and scowled" upon—to the "love and veneration" which greeted his return in death, the newspaper insisted: "Yesterday witnessed the real triumphal march of Abraham Lincoln; for he had conquered the prejudices of all hordes and classes. . . . Better for his fame that it should come thus late than too soon."

"New York never before saw such a day," the *Herald* insisted. Neither had Abraham Lincoln. One senses that if he had given New York a chance, he might have.[36]

---

[36] Freeman, *Abraham Lincoln Comes to New York*, 111–12; *New York Herald*, April 26, 1865.

2

The Volcano Under the City: The Significance of Draft Rioting in New York City and State, July 1863

Iver Bernstein

IN JULY 1863, at a crucial turning point in the Civil War, armed mobs halted the effort of the Lincoln administration to conduct the first federal draft and virtually took over New York City in what was to become the bloodiest urban riot in American history. When the last crowds were scattered after four days of violence, at least 105 people were dead and possibly many more. Along with the death toll, the citywide scale of the violence and the range of targets went well beyond what antebellum urban mobs had contemplated. Rioters attacked not only draft offices and officials but also an array of individuals and installations associated with the Republican Party and Lincoln's national government, as well as abolitionist leaders, Protestant reform agencies, and now, six months after the Emancipation Proclamation, the city's relatively defenseless African-American community. At times the riots almost seemed to be a distinct battle in the war—mobs raided armories for weapons and destroyed telegraph lines, railroads, ferries and bridges. The uprising ended in a series of titanic armed confrontations on the city's industrial Upper East Side in which Union troops, battle-weary from Gettysburg, retook poor Irish Catholic districts in the manner of war zones.

Irish Americans dominated the crowds, but many Irish New Yorkers stayed aloof from or fought against the mobs, and not all rioters were Irish. What was notable about the Irish mobs by the end of the first day and through the end of the insurrection was their extremism in racial and political terms. In some cases, their racist efforts to drive African-American men from the city's black enclaves culminated in grotesque lynch murders and the sexual mutilations and burnings of victims' bodies. The rioters' political gestures included cheers for Confederate President Jefferson Davis and efforts not only to barricade specific neighborhoods against advancing federal troops but to sever neighborhoods and even the city itself symbolically from the entire Northern war effort. In these doings, rioters were both acting out the suggestions of "Peace" or "Copperhead" Democratic leaders and going way beyond what even the most vitriolic party orator could have imagined.

What interested me, in preparing my 1990 book on the riots, is where this "volcano under the city," as one contemporary observer aptly described it, came from.[1] How do we account for its enormities of bloodshed, its geographic scale and ideological scope, its extremities of racial hatred and political ambition, all new in the context of mid-nineteenth-century urban social and political relations? What relation did events in New York City have to draft resistance elsewhere—for instance, the outbreak in Troy, New York, on July 15, two days after the eruption in New York City? If, as I contend, New York City's insurrection exposed and embodied a deeper set of ruptures in urban social and political life, to what extent and how were these profound problems of rule and relations resolved? The riots present an unusual opportunity to probe the ideological connections between a dramatic event and much longer-term and often quieter social processes—riot week issues of loyalty and treason made the episode a highly self-conscious one, forcing even the most neutral of observers to choose sides. The insurrection elicited lengthy commentaries on local and national racial, ethnic and class relations, party policies, neighborhood dynamics, national politics and the progress of the war, in diaries and private correspondence as well as public sources such as newspapers and court records.

---

[1] I thank Harold Holzer and the participants in the June 1999 symposium, "The Union Preserved: New York and the Civil War," for their commentary.

Iver Bernstein, *The New York City Draft Riots: Their Significance for American Society and Politics in the Age of the Civil War* (New York: Oxford University Press, 1990); William Osborn Stoddard, *The Volcano Under the City. By a Volunteer Special* (New York, 1887). The description and analysis of the Draft Riots in the discussion that follows derive, in large part, from my Oxford University Press book, *The New York City Draft Riots*, cited above.

What made such questions about the origins, dynamics, and implications of the Draft Riots particularly urgent and arresting was my realization that the episode represented a kind of lost history of the Civil War. Here was an event that was deeply embarrassing to all involved, particularly as the Union war effort took on the momentum and inevitability of a winning cause in the months following. The memory of the insurrection would surface in subsequent moments of labor strife, social crisis, or race panic—1872, 1877, 1886—but by the turn of the century, it had drifted out of the consciousness of most New Yorkers and Americans (with the exception of the New York City police, whose bravery and successful rallying during the riots became a long-lasting source of institutional pride). Certainly the disloyalty and racism of the draft rioters hung like an ominous and acrid cloud over the North's efforts to do justice to the African American former slaves during Reconstruction. What kind of commitment to racial justice in the South was a North that could produce such grotesque riots capable of?[2] To take the Draft Riots seriously, then, may require some qualification of the triumphal narrative of a unified North marching to freedom in the Civil War—a triumphal narrative that may well be inescapable and at some level we may all share.

At the heart of the Draft Riots were two related identity crises— New York City's problematic relation to the United States (itself undergoing a profound crisis of identity during the era of the Civil War), and New York's own intramural problem of identity, coherence, and community. Before the Civil War, New York was the Northern capital of proslavery and pro-Southern sentiment, in some ways, a kind of Northern outpost of the slave empire. Slavery had flourished in New York through the eighteenth century, and while it was not a colony made for slavery, like South Carolina, it had a higher proportion of black residents than any colony north of Delaware. Slavery ended legally in New York State with the general emancipation of 1827, but the city's merchants continued to finance the southern slave owners' flourishing cotton trade. Some of those merchants were even involved in the illegal Atlantic slave market, which most mid-nineteenth-century Americans regarded as the most extreme form of

---

[2] See Eric Foner, *Reconstruction: America's Unfinished Revolution* (New York: Harper & Row, 1988), ch. 1.

barbarism. As late as 1860, the illegal ships, or "Blackbirders," arrived in New York port and continued to receive the surprisingly open sanction of New York's customhouse officials, federal judges, and juries.[3]

The continuing power of slavery in the city was well known by local black leader William Powell. He had led a mass meeting of black New Yorkers against the Fugitive Slave Law of 1850 in which he advocated physical resistance if black homes were invaded in the enforcement of the law. Powell's Globe Hotel was invaded in July 1863, not by proslavery kidnappers but by Irish rioters in search of black targets. (Powell's preparedness from the heyday of the Fugitive Slave Law served him well: in 1863 he rigged a bo'sun's chair that carried him and his household a hundred feet across the tenement rooftops to a place where they could flee the crowds and board a boat to the safe haven of New Bedford, Massachusetts.)[4]

In the secession winter of 1860–61, the mayor of New York City, Fernando Wood, suggested to the municipal government (with the support of some leading citizens) that the city secede from the Union at the same moment that South Carolina and other Lower South states were withdrawing, and set itself up as a free commercial republic so as to keep its trade with the slave South and England undiminished. The plan was defeated, and New York City would remain loyal to the Union during the Civil War, but shrewdly, the Lincoln administration never took its loyalty for granted.

If New York was, from one angle of vision, a "Southern" city, then, from another, related perspective, it was a "white" city, the Northern

---

[3] On New York City's relationship to slavery, both as a site for Northern slavery before 1827 and as an outpost of a Southern slave empire, see Ira Berlin, *Many Thousands Gone: The First Two Centuries of Slavery in North America* (Cambridge, MA: Harvard University Press, 1998); Winthrop Jordan, *White Over Black: American Attitudes Towards The Negro, 1550–1812* (Chapel Hill: University of North Carolina Press, 1968); Phillip Foner, *Business & Slavery: New York Merchants and the Irrepressible Conflict* (Chapel Hill: University of North Carolina Press, 1941); Shane White, *Somewhat More Independent: The End of Slavery in New York City, 1770–1810* (Athens, GA: University Press of Georgia, 1991); Ernest A. McKay, *The Civil War and New York City* (Syracuse: Syracuse University Press, 1990); see also Joanne Pope Melish, *Discovering Slavery: Gradual Emancipation and "Race" in New England, 1780–1860* (Ithaca: Cornell University Press, 1998).

[4] For a discussion of Powell, see George E. Walker, *The Afro-American in New York City, 1827–1860* (New York: Garland Publishing, 1993), 24–25, 56, 71–72, 125, 173–74; Adrian Cook, *The Armies of the Streets: The New York City Draft Riots of 1863* (Lexington, KY: University Press of Kentucky, 1974), 80.

nerve center of a newly formalized and so-called scientific "white" ideology. No one spoke more vociferously for this emergent outlook than John H. Van Evrie, physician, journalist, and sometime political correspondent of Jefferson Davis, through his white supremacist newspaper, the New York *Weekly Caucasian* and proslavery screeds such as *Negroes and Negro "Slavery": The First an Inferior Race— The Latter its Normal Condition*, first published in 1853, revised and expanded during the first year of the war. Van Evrie wrote for an Irish Catholic audience devastated by poverty. With the move of Archbishop John Hughes from Philadelphia to New York by the 1840s, it could be argued that New York had replaced its neighbor to the south as the American capital of the Catholic Church and its broad and growing constituency of famine Irish immigrants. The position of these poor Irish women and men was deeply ambiguous.

In many ways the 1850s and 60s was the moment when the Irish first gained significant political power in New York through their presence in the Democratic Party and the labor movement. Their political aspirations were stunningly articulated by Archbishop Hughes in lectures such as the widely reprinted *The Decline Of Protestantism, And Its Cause*, first delivered at St. Patrick's in 1850. "Every body should know that we have for our mission to convert the world,—including the inhabitants of the United States,—the people of the cities . . . the Legislatures, the Senate, the Cabinet, the President, and all," Hughes announced.[5] But this expansive theological and political confidence was hard to sustain. New York's Irish Catholics retained their commitment to the tight-knit *clachan* or traditional Irish village, whose crowding was, Peter Quinn observes, retained in New York City not just out of necessity but also out of choice. Here the emphasis was not on expansive engagement with the encountered culture but secession into what Quinn aptly calls the "sodalities" of church and saloon life.[6] And even on the theological front, Irish Catholics' confidence ebbed: many felt that the best response to what they perceived as the corrosive subjectivity of Protestants' "private interpretation" of the Bible was separation and withdrawal, not engagement. The dominant American culture repudiated Irish Catholic

---

[5] John Hughes, *The Decline Of Protestantism, And Its Cause* (New York: Edward Duncan & Bro., 1850), 26.

[6] Peter Quinn, "Farmers No More: From Rural Ireland to the Teeming City," in Michael Coffey, ed., *The Irish in America* (New York: Hyperion 1997), 41–42.

efforts to advance, through the harsh nativism of the Know Nothing movement and the hate-filled cartoons and slurs that portrayed Irish Americans and African Americans as sub-human and animalistic. Both groups were described as "lazy," "bestial," "low-browed," and "simian." Even an educated observer such as lawyer George Templeton Strong was not above making such racial comparisons, referring to what he dubbed the "prehensile paws" of Irish workmen and denouncing the "Celtic beast" while proclaiming that "Southern Cuffee seems of a higher social grade than Northern paddy."[7] There was a deep anxiety, not surprisingly, in the experience of the newly arrived Irish that explains the readiness with which many of them defined themselves as members of a "white" master race and entertained Van Evrie and other Democratic propagandists' pseudo-scientific assertions about America as a "white man's country" that had no place for blacks, considered biologically separate and hence a "permanently inferior" species.[8] If the Irish were only tenuously American, they felt that at least they were somehow "above" their black neighbors by virtue of skin color.

Of course, such efforts to imagine or invent a "white city" ignored rich ironies and powerful realities. Many African-American New Yorkers could trace their local lineage well back before the American Revolution, if not earlier. Especially after Emancipation, Democratic orators fanned anxieties among Irish audiences that newly freed and "low wage" blacks would flood north to steal Irish jobs, but such fears were never realized. Indeed, Irish Americans had crowded out African-American workers from their foothold in the unskilled sector of the New York economy in the 1840s and 50s. And for all the efforts of the Irish Longshoreman's Union and the Democratic Party to advocate separation of "superior" "white" Irish from "low-wage" and "inferior" blacks, Irish and black men and women and families mixed, were often intimate, and sometimes married. Such mixing was especially common along the waterfront.

If New York was from one vantage an outpost of the slave empire and a "white" city, it could also make claim to being a capital of the Northern antislavery and benevolent empire, a center of what the

---

[7] Allan Nevins and Milton Halsey Thomas, eds., *The Diary of George Templeton Strong*, 3 vols. (New York: Macmillan, 1952), 3: 342, 245.

[8] J[ohn]. H. Van Evrie, M.D., *Negroes and Negro "Slavery," The First, An Inferior Race—The Latter, Its Normal Condition* (Baltimore: John D. Toy, 1853).

draft rioters and their sympathizers would call "Black Republican-ism." Horace Greeley's abolitionist newspaper, the *Daily Tribune*, dubbed the "political bible of the North," made its home there, as did the philanthropic dynamos, the Tappan brothers, and the brilliant black abolitionist Henry Highland Garnet; meanwhile, over in Brook-lyn, that oracle of moral enterprise, Henry Ward Beecher, was hold-ing forth. In New York City, too, could be found the agencies of the United States Sanitary Commission and a host of other benevolent secular or Protestant enterprises.

The Draft Riots in New York, then, were the outgrowth of these identity crises—a divided New York's relationship with a divided America and especially the deeply uneasy relation of New York's parts to each other. The Civil War and particularly the situation in early summer 1863 brought these issues of identity and community into focus with an unbearable intensity. The small Republican elite in the city saw the war as an extraordinary opportunity for consolidat-ing its power and expanding its influence. The war provided momen-tum to the project of immediate emancipation of four million enslaved African Americans and to the related project of political centralization, expanding the activities of the federal government in the name of moral reform. The Republicans' reform ventures could now be advanced simultaneously on the local and the new national stages. For the city's opposing Democratic majority—its until-re-cently-Southern-leaning merchants, its newly Americanizing immi-grant population (over half of the city's total population was foreign-born by 1855) and its powerful Catholic clergy and politicos—the war required a far more complex and perilous negotiation with the newly ascendant forces of antislavery and wartime nationalism. Arch-bishop Hughes was a committed Unionist; early in the war, he even served as Lincoln's delegate to Europe to plead the Northern cause. But Hughes and the city's Catholic clergy were vehement opponents of abolitionism, which they saw as the American manifestation of Europe's "lawless" revolutionary liberalism and theological heresy—the abolitionists were "Deists, Atheists, Pantheists, anything but Christian," as one Catholic orator put it. Many of New York's poorer Catholics perceived the post-emancipation war as a violation of the terms of an implicit agreement with the national government set out at the beginning of the fighting in 1861 and of their understanding of what it meant to be an American: they would fight to restore the

Union but not to end slavery and, by extension, to raise the status of African Americans.

The Lincoln administration's Conscription Act of March 1863 heightened such Irish Catholic perceptions that the purposes of the war had been perverted. The Act was passed at a bleak moment in the fortunes of the Union Army, after its debacle at Fredericksburg. (Indeed, the whole direction of the war in spring and early summer 1863 was exceedingly unclear and open-ended—both on the battle-field and with regards to enforcement of the draft. General George Meade was perhaps not exaggerating when he declared in a letter on July 16 that he "always had expected the crisis of this revolution to turn on the attempt to execute the conscription act," and three weeks later, "if the draft is not heartily responded to, the Government had better make up its mind to letting the South go.")[9] The March Act subjected all men between 20 and 35 and all unmarried men be-tween 35 and 45 to military duty. Names were procured through a laborious house-to-house enrollment conducted by government agents. Then a lottery in each congressional district determined who would go to war. The most controversial provision allowed drafted men to provide substitutes or buy their way out of service for $300. Though intended to put a ceiling on the price of a substitute, the $300 clause was perceived by many poor New York Democrats as an effort to transfer the burden of the war to straitened immigrant labor-ers. The discriminatory draft law—passed at a moment of high uncer-tainty in the direction of the war, giving the Lincoln government new powers of summary arrest through its Provost Marshal Bureau, its quotas of drafted men rumored to be disproportionately high for New York State and City, and scheduled to be enforced after a long spring of inflation and labor agitation—had the effect of triggering a social panic among the city's immigrant and Catholic poor. As the law pertained to "citizens" of the United States, theoretically only whites were subject to the draft. Did the law thus conceal a Republican conspiracy to sweep Catholic Democratic workers (and voters) into the carnage at the front and fill their jobs with the cheap labor of newly emancipated slaves? Democratic orators fanned such fears, moving from Hughes's anti-abolitionism to an extreme proslavery po-

---

[9] Meade quoted in Jack Franklin Leach, *Conscription in the United States: Histor-ical Background* (Rutland, VT: C. E. Tuttle, 1952), 347.

sition that translated Van Evrie's pseudo-scientific racism into the language of the gutter. Wartime nationalism had polarized and clarified the differences between Republican and Democratic elites and between Republican and Democratic followers. Now the draft, biased against the poor, magnifying white racial fears, involving the federal government as never before in local affairs, made preexisting conflicts seem even more real and hysterically urgent. Governor Seymour's July Fourth speech helped create the mood of an imminent release of tensions: if the needs of justice could not be carried out through constitutional means, he remarked, by repealing or amending the discriminatory draft act, the same purposes could and would be accomplished by a mob.

The first draft lottery in New York City was carried out peacefully on Saturday, July 11. That hot weekend, the names of the first drafted men replaced the long lists of city residents who had died at Gettysburg as front-page news, and New Yorkers pondered the fact that Seymour and other Democratic leaders had not been able to block the draft. Whatever limited planning the coming violence had seems to have taken place in saloons, kitchens, and street corners on Sunday the twelfth; rumor and circumstance and not orchestration and premeditation would dominate the events to come.

The riots began Monday morning the thirteenth, not at the hour of the resumption of the draft lottery (scheduled for 10:30 A.M.), but at the hour of work. Between 6 and 7 A.M., employees of the city's railroads, machine shops, and shipyards, iron foundry workers, "hundreds of others employed in buildings and street improvements" failed to appear at their jobs; they streamed up the city's uptown avenues, closing shops, factories, and construction sites, urging workmen along the way to join the procession. This was the usual style for a strike action in the mid-nineteenth century, the way strikers informed others (who often did not speak their language) of a work stoppage. After a brief meeting at Central Park, the crowd, women and men both represented, broke into two columns, and with "No Draft" placards held aloft, marched downtown to the draft office at Third Avenue and 47th Street, at the edges of the immigrant tenement district, scene of the scheduled lottery. In some Monday morning episodes, self-deputized "committees" of workers visited employers and peaceably advised them to close down for the day; in others, rioters began to hack down telegraph poles—one reporter overheard such a crowd discussing the need to prevent authorities from summoning troops from Albany. Irish women used crowbars to pull up the tracks of northbound railroads; still another mob of Irish men and women attacked Superintendent of Police John A. Kennedy, spotted out of uniform. Kennedy was chased, caught, dragged through the mud and beaten on the head until almost "unrecognizable."

At 10:30, draft selection began inside the Provost Marshal's office while a crowd waited on the street. After some names had been drawn, the firemen of the appropriately named Black Joke Engine Company pulled up to the office in full fire regalia. One of the Black Joke men had been drafted in Saturday's lottery, and the volunteer fire companies believed their traditional exemption from militia service should extend to the draft. Led by the firemen, the throng outside burst in, smashed the lottery wheel, and set the building on fire. By 11:30 that first morning, orders were given to suspend the draft in the affected districts.

After Monday noon, concourses of hundreds of men, women, and children milled about the uptown avenues enjoying the holiday from business, debating the draft and discussing the disturbance and its direction. One cohort paid a friendly visit to Democratic General George B. McClellan's house. Shortly after noon, rioters appeared at Printing House Square, the journalistic thoroughfare, huzzahed McClellan and the offices of Democratic newspapers, and groaned at those of the Republican papers, especially Horace Greeley's *Tribune*. There were murderous threats against the abolitionist Greeley himself, some in the crowd searching for the editor's cherubic face and telltale white overcoat, but the crowd resisted the urgings to violence and dispersed when Greeley failed to appear.

Meanwhile the pattern of violence increasingly reflected the more violent of Monday morning's activities. The deserted 8th District draft office was burned at 5:00 P.M. Monday by an Irish cellar digger and an estimated 300 men and boys. Elsewhere policemen caught by the rioters were stripped of their clothing and literally defaced. Now these attacks were joined by others against expensive Republican homes in which picture frames, furniture, pianos, and bed clothes were destroyed; well-dressed gentlemen were accosted on the street and robbed (sometimes $300 was referred to). By suppertime, one mob had set fire to the splendid Colored Orphan Asylum on Fifth Avenue and another began attacking and in one instance lynching black men and boys in the tenements along the downtown water-front. Crowds returned to Greeley's *Tribune* in the early evening, stormed through the offices and tried to burn them down. Monday evening we find the earliest evidence of rioters who had clearly par-ticipated in the early protest against the draft now abandoning the crowds and joining the patrols and fire companies to guard property. Tuesday morning, the rioters who returned to the streets and re-sumed the battle against the police—these rioters were more predict-ably Irish and Catholic, young and male, and employed in the foundries, railroad shops, and construction and dock gangs that clus-tered in the waterfront and in the uptown industrial wards. (In this and other regards, there was some parallel to the riot on Wednesday the fifteenth that overtook Troy, New York, and halted the draft, de-stroyed a Republican newspaper office, stripped German brothels, partially ruined a black church, and sent African-American families fleeing into the hills; the Irish molders and nail factory workers in the Troy uprising resembled in ethnic and occupational profile these New York City rioters.)[10] The native and German workers and skilled artisans who were also on the streets of New York City Monday morning largely disappear from riot accounts and arrest records by Tuesday. The violence on Tuesday and Wednesday was characterized by attacks on other draft offices (indeed, concern with the specter of the draft remained ever present) and titanic struggles between huge, heavily Irish crowds and the police and military. Indeed, by Wednes-day, troops began to arrive in the city from Gettysburg.

Wednesday also witnessed the grisly onslaught of young Irish men against black families and black homes, and especially black men, in the city's scattered African-American enclaves. In one of eleven recorded lynch killings from July 13 to 15, Abraham Franklin, a crip-pled black coachman, was pulled from his house by an Irish-led mob and hanged from a lamppost. The approach of troops scattered the rioters and the soldiers cut Franklin down. As soon as the military left, the murderous crew reappeared, hanged Franklin's body from the lamppost again, with cheers for "Jeff Davis." Later the body was taken down again, and Patrick Butler, a sixteen-year-old Irish

---

[10] For an account of the Troy riot, see E. H. G. Clark, *The Trojan Mob: A Plain Statement* (Troy, NY, np, 1863; copy in Troy Public Library); Leach, *Conscription in the United States*, 319–20.

butcher, grabbed Franklin's body by the genitals and pulled it through the streets as bystanders yelled approval. Here the relation between Irish Americans and African Americans was played out in all its tragic complexity, hatred being the dominant message but sexual lure serving as a kind of leitmotif. White abolitionist Mattie Griffith described the acts of unimaginable cruelty committed upon the city's black population during the midweek violence: "A child of 3 years of age was thrown from a 4th story window and instantly killed. A woman one hour after her confinement was set upon and beaten with her tender babe in her arms. Children were torn from their mother's embrace and their brains blown out in the very face of the afflicted mother. Men were burnt by slow fires."[11]

The city's black community was in some instances able to defend itself from this pogrom: there is one known instance of armed black people defending themselves from a rooftop, and others of horrified and sympathetic whites interceding to help black victims. William Powell's ingenious escape, already noted, was accomplished with the help of a neighboring Jewish family. Many other black families fled Manhattan to the surrounding countryside.

The riot ended late on Thursday as federal troops deployed howitzers to sweep aside the barricades the rioters had constructed in the uptown neighborhoods. As the violence reached a desperate intensity on some barricaded Upper East Side blocks, mobs searched tenements for wounded "enemy" soldiers, while soldiers combed buildings for rioters, who, when found, were driven off the rooftops. In the red heat of Wednesday's and Thursday's violence, there were scattered assaults against Chinese peddlers; attacks against the white wives of men of color; a sacking of Brooks Brothers' clothing store; and the smashing of brothels, in the tradition of European revolutionary mobs. The final act in the drama was Archbishop John Hughes's speech to the crowd from the steps of his home on Friday, July 17. There was no need for a revolution on the streets, Hughes was reported to have said—in America we have a revolution at the ballot box every four years. The Catholic leader, who could still command a reverent hearing among the Irish laity, hoped to convey his

---

[11] Mattie Griffith to Mary Estlin, N.Y., July 27, 1863, Estlin Papers, Dr. Williams's Library, London, England. I thank Eric Foner for bringing this letter to my attention.

empathy for the widespread anti-draft sentiment while urging upon his listeners this ringing endorsement of the legal forms of American democracy. When the Archbishop finished, his audience dispersed without help from the troops posted nearby.

The riot-week crisis of authority was exacerbated by the deep disagreement among city leaders over whether to declare federal martial law and establish a Republican standing army in New York. As the riot expanded on Tuesday and Wednesday, it became obvious that there was no agreed strategy to restore order. To some extent, military rule was a party issue: the Republican-led Union League Club, the ultra-nationalist businessmen's club, was in favor of martial law, and Democratic financiers and politicians such as August Belmont, General McClellan, Samuel Barlow, and others were opposed.

But the debate over martial law also reflected profound differences in outlook, especially as the insurrection evolved into a gruesome race riot. The Union Leaguers and Republicans excoriated the Irish rioters (George Templeton Strong wrote, "For myself, personally, I would like to see war made on the Irish scum as in 1688.") Conversely, these Union League Republicans focused philanthropic attentions on black victims and vowed to enforce the draft at all costs. E. H. G. Clark, a Troy abolitionist who wrote about his city's "Trojan Mob" of that week, captured the essence of this Republican position: "The spirit of the mob in Troy was of course the same that impelled the bludgeon and lit the firebrand in New York, and ground into blood and dust, the most helpless and unoffending of the American people in that almost foreign city. It was simply the indirect offspring of slavery and rebellion."[12] From this viewpoint, New York City (and Troy) had been turned into wholly "foreign" cities by the Irish draft rioters and their Southern-sympathizing political allies; their treason could be contrasted with the true Americanism of the riot's African-American victims.

By contrast, Democrats such as August Belmont and his circle negotiated with the white rioters, ignored black victims, and sought to have the draft overturned in the courts. While the pro-martial law wing condemned the Irish Catholic draft rioters as an "unworthy poor," undeserving of charity and best persuaded by force, they were opposed by anti-martial law Democrats who thought that same white immigrant

---

[12] Clark, *Trojan Mob*, 1.

poor eminently worthy of charity—*they* were the victims. The Tammany Democracy thus proposed to neutralize the draft by a massive public appropriation to pay the commutation fees of poor men. The riots thus highlighted the relative absence of consensus among the "better classes" over basic questions of social and political rule.

Immigrant New York's problematic relation to America and the national government, and the problem of political and social community within the city, had suddenly become fused in a profound crisis of authority. Would New York City be confirmed as a Northern City? A Southern City? Or, indeed, a "white" city where African Americans had no public rights or role? Or, perhaps, a "Black Republican" city where African Americans could confidently claim freedom of travel and other civil rights as well as political voice? In this way, the issue of July 1863 was the wartime reconstruction of New York City.

Lincoln did not declare martial law, despite frantic letters from New York Republicans urging him to place the city under the dictatorial General Benjamin Butler (whom Southerners had nicknamed "the Beast"). Instead, he appointed General John Adams Dix—an old Jacksonian Democrat and financier who had the confidence of both ultra-nationalist Union Leaguers and the Democratic capitalists of the Belmont stripe—as military commander of the Department of the East. Dix would succeed, one month later, in carrying off the draft lotteries without martial law. But the most important event to insure the return of peace to New York City was the confirmation of Boss William M. Tweed's Tammany Hall as the city's premier Democratic organization. Tammany's pre-riot record as patriotic defender of the war made it the direct beneficiary of post-riot indignation against treasonous rioters and politicians. Tammany officials stood watch at the peaceful August draft lotteries. Tammany's ultimate trump was a "County Loan" ordinance, administered by Tweed and a bipartisan committee, which paid the $300 draft waiver for poor conscripts who could not find an acceptable substitute. The Committee encouraged drafted men to visit the many agents who supplied substitutes for a fee, if indeed the Tammany Supervisors did not hire the services of brokers directly. Tammany's County Loan ordinance virtually guaranteed that poor conscripts who did not care to serve would not be compelled to do so, and also that the army would get its men, or at least its quota, from New York City.

The problem of building community out of this disorder, even of determining winners and losers, was a daunting one, and was hardly resolved by the military victory of the Union Army on the Upper East Side or the successful August draft lottery. The Republicans and President Lincoln got some of what they wanted: the riot did not spread, the draft continued, the North went on to win the war—and the Republicans got the credit. But on closer examination, the Republican "victory" over the rioters also had elements of concession and defeat. The failure to declare martial law in the city suggested that the most radical Republicans would have their hands tied when they finally came to national power after the war. The Radical Republicans' brief tenure in Washington from 1866 to 1868 would allow them license to proceed with military reconstruction only in the South, not in New York City. A more clear-cut case can be made for the victory of Democratic business leaders, who at least would be allowed to run local affairs without Republican interference. But the riots and their aftermath demonstrated that fashionable millionaires such as Belmont and Barlow would retain power in the city only if they acknowledged the claims of Boss Tweed's "Ring" of Tammany politicians who sat on the Board of Supervisors and presided over the draft exemption fund. If the Draft Riots represented a triumph for the Democratic elite, it was one riddled with major concessions to Tweed and Tammany.

Boss Tweed and Tammany's successful post-riot political arrangement demands closer attention—certainly Tweed emerged from the riots in a position of power. Loyal nationalism was the *sine qua non* of Tweed's formula. No one, not even the super patriots of the Union League Club, could match the histrionic flag-waving and hoarse cheering of a Tammany Hall Fourth of July celebration in the mid-1860s. After the riots, Tammany's patriotic commitment to the Union war effort served as evidence of the loyalty of a broad segment of immigrant voters in Democratic New York City. Even the ultra-elitist George Templeton Strong reluctantly supported Tammany after the Draft Riots as the middle ground between a controversial and impotent local Republican Party and what he perceived as the treasonous and riotous *canaille* who supported the Southern-sympathizing Fernando Wood.

Tammany-style loyal nationalism, more important still, was appealing to the many Irish-American men and women who hoped to offer some confirmation of their loyalty after the Draft Riots. For an Irish lower middle class striving to lose the taint of proletarian treason, the stylish Tammany Mayor A. Oakey Hall became the emblem of a domain of bourgeois fashion and sensibility open for the first time to the Irish community. Hall believed himself a great literateur; one sympathetic listener imagined that "his first message as Mayor, in point of perspicuity and attractiveness, might have been written by Thackeray." To polish this image of cultivation and elegance, Oakey even submitted his own custom jewelry designs at Tiffany's. He nonetheless still fancied himself as a man of the people—in one of his early acts as mayor he abolished the traditional salutation, "Your Honor." The Harvard-educated Hall was not Irish (though he played up a story that a maternal ancestor was one of the regicides of Charles I—the Irish community looked with favor on a man descended from the killer of an English king). But Hall, one of the prosecutors of the draft rioters in New York City, did everything otherwise possible to clothe himself in sentiments of loyal Irish Americanism. He was fond of joking with Irish audiences that his initials A.O.H. stood for the "Ancient Order of Hibernians." One Irish observer remembered the Saint Patrick's Day Parade of 1870 as a high moment of Oakey's career. As Tammany Irish dignitaries Sweeny, Connolly, Richard O'Gorman and the city's Irish societies passed Hall's reviewing stand, the mayor saluted "in the supposed regalia of an Irish Prince. It was not enough for him to put a shamrock on the lapel of his coat . . . to adequately typify his consuming love for the 'Exiles of Erin,' he wore a coat of green material and a flourishing cravat of the same inspiring color." When he attended the lavish 1870 Annual Ball of Tweed's Americus Club in green fly-tail coat, green kids, green shirt embroidered with shamrocks and emeralds, and eye-glasses "with rims of Irish bog-oak and attached to a green silk cord," Hall's unmistakable message was that "Irishness" was now acceptable in New York society. For those Irish men and women seeking inclusion in the world of elite nationalism after the Civil War, Hall's antic display provided a sense of legitimacy, of the Americanization of the Irish.

Perhaps the most crucial element of Tammany's post-war appeal was its emphasis on white supremacy. Even though the Union League Club succeeded in integrating the city's streetcars and marched the newly-created African-American 20th Regiment down Broadway after the riots, the size of the city's black population, declining since the 1830s, would drop by nearly a third over the course of the war. No doubt the riots had much to do with that shift. A post-riot climate of intimidation and fear made the public life of the city a more noticeably white domain. In this process Tammany cooperated. It drew its ideological line at acceptance of the Thirteenth Amendment abolishing slavery, and vehemently opposed the two subsequent amendments to establish constitutional rights to black citizenship and suffrage. In the context of the debate over Irish and black status that the Draft Riots put in sudden focus, the message of Mayor Hall and Tammany was confirmation of the whiteness and loyalty of the Irish and the clear demarcation of the riots' black victims as an inferior and degraded race—by implication, un-American—who were not worthy of organized philanthropy.

The tragedy of the Draft Riot and its denouement under Tammany was that they suggest how essential such brutal schemes of racial inclusion and exclusion would continue to be to the governing of New York and to the resolving of the city's problematic relationship to America. By 1870, black chattel slavery in the United States was dead and New York's labor movement had begrudgingly endorsed the principles of black citizenship and suffrage (though this is hardly to say that anti-black racism was ebbing). Revealingly, it was at just this juncture that A. Oakey Hall and Tammany allied with Irish and German labor leaders to stage a Workingmen's Anti-Chinese rally. The centerpiece of the event was Hall's reading of a letter from labor leader John Swinton, describing the Chinese as an "inferior type" of humanity, bringing paganism, incest, sodomy, and the threat of miscegenation to American shores. This distorted echo of the Draft Riots lacked sufficient impact to influence long-term political loyalties and the fear of an invasion of Chinese laborers quickly subsided. However, the workingmen's anti-Chinese movement in New York made clear, further and in another form, the resilience of racial hierarchy, prejudice, and exclusion in Northern urban life, after slavery and its particular requirements of racial caste had been abolished. Even after slavery it was extraordinarily and tragically difficult to create or even imagine a political order in the urban North that could consolidate and manage rapid change and growth, reconcile the city's foreign-ness and its American-ness (and incorporate an immigrant working class increasingly conscious of its power), and do so without a ruthless scheme of racial exclusion. New York, it could be said, had been confirmed as a Northern city, but indeed, as such, it was a precursor of the still not fully reconstructed North we know today.

3

What's Gender Got to Do With It?: New York in the Age of Civil War

Lillian Serece Williams

NEW YORK played a major role in the Civil War on the on the home front, as well as on the battlefield. It was the largest and wealthiest state in the Union and by the war's end it had contributed more soldiers, money, and supplies to the effort than had any other state.[1] The war in New York actually began to take shape long before the 1861 Confederate attack on Fort Sumter, South Carolina.

New York had been the site of several conventions that addressed issues of freedom and states' rights that were played out during the course of the war. The New York Anti-Slavery Convention of 1837 highlighted the inequities that free blacks experienced in the North and the hypocrisy of Northern attacks on the South because of its racial atrocities. The Free Soil Party held its 1848 convention in Buffalo, New York and committed itself to "free soil, free speech, free labor, and free men." The National Negro Convention movement also held several meetings in the state. In Buffalo in 1843, a spirited debate between Frederick Douglass of Rochester and the Reverend Henry Highland Garnet of Troy ensued and delegates pursued a more militant stance towards abolition, while they simultaneously sought to guarantee the rights of citizenship to free blacks.[2] In 1864

---

[1] New York contributed nearly one-fourth of the men and one-half of the money. Governor James Wadsworth gubernatorial campaign, 1862. Broadside SCO BD 152–153; A3063, NYS Manuscript Collection.

[2] Howard H. Bell, "National Convention of Colored Men, Held at Buffalo, 1843," in *Proceedings of the National Negro Convention, 1830–1864* (New York: Arno Press and *The New York Times*, 1969).

delegates meeting in Syracuse still decried the atrocities that blacks were continuing to experience and called for freedom and equality.[3]

James McPherson, Noah Andre Trudeau, Allen Ballard, Joseph Glathaar, and other scholars have documented the subsequent participation of African-American men in Union war efforts. However, they have paid little attention to the impact that the war played in redefining gender and gender roles.[4] The process by which African Americans were enlisted in the armed forces was a protracted one that raises a number of issues surrounding manhood and who could engage in manly activities. Manhood was characterized by a patriarchy in which men headed their families, displayed noble principles, manifested reason and intellect, governed, voted, and waged war. For substantial numbers of African Americans, slavery made it difficult, if not impossible, for them to head their families or to support them.[5] Free blacks lived in a state of quasi-freedom that gave them all of the responsibilities of citizenship, but few of its benefits. For example, in the election of 1862 New Yorkers defeated the suffrage bill that would have enfranchised blacks and instead elected a Democratic governor and Democratic-controlled legislature that opposed Lincoln's policy of extending the war and emancipation.[6]

Blacks had effectively been excluded from the military throughout the North by the National Militia Act of 1795. Although they had fought in all United States wars, they had no official status and they reaped few rewards for their efforts. White men persistently resisted black men's efforts to form militias and to volunteer to fight in the Civil War. Some contended that this was a "white man's war" and that there was no place for blacks. From the early days of the war the

---

[3] "National Convention of Colored Men, Held in the City of Syracuse, N.Y., 1864, in ibid.

[4] James McPherson, *The Negro's Civil War* (New York: Vintage, 1965); Hans L. Trefousse, *The Radical Republicans: Lincoln's Vanguard for Racial Justice* (New York: Alfred A. Knopf, 1969); Noah Andre Trudeau, *Like Men of War: Black Troops in the Civil War 1862–1865* (Boston: Little, Brown, 1998); Allen Ballard, *Where I'm Bound* (New York: Simon & Schuster, 2000).

[5] See Aldon Morris in the foreword to Darlene Clark Hine and Ernestine Jenkins, *A Question of Manhood* (Bloomington: Indiana University Press, 1999), xi–xii.

[6] Leon Litwack, *North of Slavery* (Chicago: University of Chicago Press, 1961). Pivotal election in New York, "Campaign for the Union 1862, Broadside 13, Manuscript and Special Collections, New York State Library; Jerome Mushkat, *The Reconstruction of the New York Democracy, 1861–1874* (Madison, NJ: Fairleigh Dickinson University Press, 1981), 70.

issue of black men's participation was questioned, despite the early defeats that the Union suffered. An 1862 *Harper's Weekly* cartoon criticized the white resistance by depicting a drowning aristocratic white man refusing the rope that a black man extends to save him because no "decent White Man is going to allow himself to be saved by a confounded n————."[7] For some to employ black soldiers meant that white soldiers were not up to the task. Felix Brannigan, a young New York private in a letter to his sister, rationalized that "we don't want to fight side by side with the n————. We think we are too superior a race."[8] For white men, then, the war raised questions about their manhood as it was socially constructed. Increasingly, Northern white men perceived slavery as incompatible with their own freedom. As the war intensified the dilemma for white men became one of either sacrificing whiteness or losing their status as free men.[9]

While the war progressed, with no apparent end in sight, the notion of arming blacks began to be debated and embraced by more whites, even in the Confederacy. Senator John Sherman wrote his brother, the general, in late August of 1862 that "men of all parties who now appreciate the magnitude of the contest, and who are determined to preserve the unity of the government at all hazards, agree that we must seek and make it the interest of the Negroes to help us."[10] Some white observers rightly noted that the Civil War would effect a social revolution as far as blacks and their manhood were concerned. In June 1863 Francis Barnes, second lieutenant in the 80th United States Colored Troops (Corps d'Afrique), served in Louisiana and was a keen observer of his troops and the politics of the war. This resident of Phoenix, Oswego County, New York, informed his wife:

> It is a grand idea—this raising a great army of Colored men to fight for their freedom and the Union. My only regret is that the policy was

---

[7] *Harper's Weekly*, August 16, 1862, 528 (app.harpweek.com).

[8] Private Felix Brannigan (74th NYSV) to his sister, quoted in Benjamin Quarles, *The Negro in the Civil War* (Boston: Little, Brown, 1953), 31.

[9] David Roediger, *The Wages of Whiteness* (New York: Verso, 1991); Noel Ignatiev, *How the Irish Became White* (New York: Routledge, 1998); Scott L. Malcomson, *One Drop of Blood* (New York: Farrar, Straus & Giroux, 2000).

[10] John Sherman to William Tecumseh Sherman, August 24, 1862, quoted in Benjamin Quarles, *The Negro in the Civil War*, 158.

not adopted long ago. . . . The mills of God grind slowly, but I think that slavery has got caught between the "upper and the nether mill-stone" this time so that it will be effectually ground out. There is no disputing the fact that negroes make good soldiers, however much some may cavil about it. . . . [T]he experiment thus far has been eminently successful. . . . At any rate it is to be thoroughly tried and that will settle the question for all time to come. It will elevate the negro to a new sphere and will make men of them instead of mere brutes.[11]

Harper's Weekly illustrated "rebel" Louisiana governor Henry Allen's call for the arming of black slaves in 1864. Allen noted further that the "conscription of Negroes should be accompanied with freedom and the privilege of remaining in the state."[12]

Prominent black spokesmen, from the outset, perceived the outbreak of the Civil War as an opportunity to achieve manhood. Frederick Douglass and other civilians responded immediately to the 1862 United States government's request to recruit "Colored" soldiers.[13] Douglass's sons Charles and Lewis were among his first recruits.[14] Blacks serving in the U. S. Colored Troops responded enthusiastically and with valor. Initially, many, such as the Douglass sons, had enlisted in the famous 54th Massachusetts regiment because New York State refused to accept them. These soldiers eventually comprised about ten percent of the troops from New York, just as they did nationwide. Lincoln and General Ulysses S. Grant and their immediate commanders all praised them for their valor and contended that the war could not have been won without their contributions.[15]

---

[11] Francis Barnes to his wife, Headquarters 2nd Division Before Port Hudson Tuesday June 23, 1863, folder 3, NYSM, SC 20332.

[12] *Harper's Weekly,* November 5, 1864, 720.

[13] Adjutant General to Frederick Douglass, August 13, 1863, Frederick Douglass papers, Manuscript Division, Library of Congress (LC), taken from the Library of Congress exhibit, *African American Odyssey.*

[14] Charles Douglass to Frederick Douglass, Readville, Camp Meigs, July 6, 1863, ibid.

[15] Thomas Wentworth Higginson, *Army Life in a Negro Regiment* (East Lansing: Michigan State University Press, 1960). Black recruits sometimes sang Tom Craig's "The Colored Volunteer," which spoke to their commitment and dedication. Broadside SCO BD 153, MSC New York State Library; Jack D. Foner, *Blacks and the Military in American History* (New York: Praeger, 1974), 48; Dudley Taylor Cornish, *The Sable Arm* (New York: W. W. Norton, 1966), frontispiece; Grant to Lincoln, August 23, 1863 in McPherson, *The Negro's Civil War,* 191. In a public letter of August 26, 1863, Lincoln reproved opponents to the use of black troops. He wrote that some black men will remember that they . . . have helped mankind on to this great consummation . . ." (Ibid., 192).

Black men expressed their views regarding the Civil War in impassioned tones at the 1864 National Convention of Colored Men that met in Syracuse. Douglass chaired the convention and noted, "The cause which we come here to promote is sacred. Nowhere in the 'wide, wide world,' can men be found coupled with a cause of greater dignity and importance than that which brings us here. . . . [L]ike all progressive races of men, we are resolved to advance in the scale of knowledge, worth, and civilization, and claim our rights among men."[16] Delegate John S. Rock reiterated Douglass's sentiment when he informed the convention that "all we ask is equal opportunities and equal rights. . . . [O]ur brave men are fighting for liberty and equality. We ask the same for the black man that is asked for the white man; nothing more, and nothing less."[17] In some ways, then, the Civil War became for white men a manifestation of their manhood and for black men a means to achieve manhood.

Just as the war challenged the meaning of manhood and expanded its definition to include blacks, the nineteenth-century notion of womanhood, characterized by domesticity, also was placed on the debate floor. Since the experiences of Southern women during the Civil War have tended to dominate the literature, we know little about the involvement of Northern women. The New York experiences offer a unique opportunity to explore questions pertaining to womanhood because of women's roles in abolition and because of its influential feminists like Susan B. Anthony and Sojourner Truth, who saw the war as an opportunity to expand the freedoms for both women and black men.[18]

When Southerners attacked Fort Sumter, Northern women wasted no time in claiming the Civil War as theirs, too. They expressed the war's importance to them and their opinions appeared in mainstream publications. The fictional character Fleta asked, "What do women know about war?" In the *Flag of Our Nation*, a Northern publication, she responded to her query thus: "What drop in all the bitter cup have they not tasted?" Fleta goes on to discuss the hardships that

---

[16] Howard Bell, Proceedings, National Convention of Colored Men held in Syracuse, October 4–7, 1864 in *Proceedings of the National Negro Convention, 1830–1864* (New York: Arno Press and *The New York Times*, 1969), 23.

[17] Ibid.

[18] See, e.g., LeeAnn Whites, *The Civil War as a Crisis in Gender* (Athens: University of Georgia, 1995).

were wrought for women as a result of the war—loneliness and despair, the agony of the loss of a loved one, the efforts required to maintain the homestead, and the anxiety they felt when they received infrequent correspondence. For Fleta this was the counterpart to man's battlefield experience.[19] Herkimer County resident Flora Avery also expressed the human toll that the war exacted on her and members of her community. She became a widow at age eighteen when her young husband was killed in the conflict. Flora Avery had lost her father-in-law in battle, too. Avery observed that "there are few families that escape the ravages of this war. They have my sympathy and that is all I can do for I feel that it is worse than useless to offer anything like consolation."[20] Avery documented the war casualties from her town, for many of their funeral services were held at her church.[21] She commented that her friend's brother-in-law was a prisoner of war in Richmond and suffered from a lack of food and clothing.[22] She later noted that "my bereavement [is] more forcefully [brought] to mind as it is my husband's birthday. One year ago today he was with me. . . . I am left alone and must spend the remainder of my days in loneliness." [23] Despite her grief, she remained committed to the Union cause.

An 1861 article in *Harper's Monthly* indicated the level of support that women gave to the war effort and, simultaneously, their views on men's participation. A heroine "drank with every breath the spirit of heroism and self-sacrifice." When her suitor chided her for knitting socks for the soldiers, she dumped him summarily and stated, "Don't, I pray you, hinder with light words even, the feeble service that a weak woman's hands may render. I am not a man, and cannot, therefore, fight for liberty and good government; but what I am able to do I am doing from a state of mind that is hurt by levity." In an 1862 *Harper's* cartoon titled "Scene on Fifth Avenue," when a young suitor informed his betrothed that he had found a substitute to replace him in the military, she registered her displeasure by sneering,

---

[19] Quoted in Alice Fahs, "The Feminized Civil War: Gender, Northern Popular Literature, and the Memory of the War, 1861–1900," in *The Journal of American History* 3 (March 1999), 1461.

[20] Flora Avery Diary, January 22, 1863, Salisbury Center, Herkimer County BD18940, MSC, New York State Library.

[21] Ibid., May 10, 1863.

[22] Ibid., December 8, 1863.

[23] Ibid., March 20, 1863.

"Have you? What a curious coincidence! And I have found one for YOU!"[24] This was a persistent theme in "Scene on Fifth Avenue." Another soldier on furlough returned to visit his ladyfriend only to be informed by a servant that she would not be available to him until Richmond had been defeated.[25]

The implications were clear. These women were imbued with the contemporary ideal of manhood and only wanted to be associated with real men. Married women embraced this definition of manhood also and took leadership in supporting the war effort, also. In an 1861 *Harper's* cartoon, a wife refused to celebrate the return of her husband from the war because he had volunteered to serve for only three months, earning this rebuke: "Get Away! No husband of mine would be here while the country needs his help."[26] Wives sometimes took the initiative to encourage reticent spouses to volunteer for military service. A "Horrified Husband" queried his butler. "What! My wife—gone! Did you say GONE?" "Yes, sar. She says she's gone Nussing to Fortress Monroe and she told me to rub up your regimentals, case you wanted to follow her."[27] White women were operating within the acceptable realm when they thus responded.

During the early years of the Republic (1776–1820) the role of elite women had been redefined. Full political identity for Americans was based upon a willingness to bear arms for the nation, as well as property ownership. Women were thought to be unfit to bear arms and married women could not exercise control over their property.[28] The ideology of the republican mother sought to redefine the role of women in a manner that emphasized that they were a part of a deeply radical republican experiment.[29] The responsibility of the republican mother, then, was to prepare her sons to serve their country. With the outbreak of the Civil War this notion prevailed and the family and community merged. Operating within this acceptable domestic sphere, the women of New York made major contributions to the war. For one thing, New York women maintained their families,

[24] *Harper's Weekly*, April 30, 1862, 560, app.harpweek.com.
[25] Ibid., August 2, 1862, 496, app.harpweek.com.
[26] Ibid., August 10, 1861, 510, app.harpweek.com.
[27] Ibid., August 16, 1862, 528, app.harpweek.com.
[28] See Peggy Rabkin, *Fathers to Daughters* (Westport, CT: Greenwood Press, reprint edition, 1981).
[29] Linda Kerber and Jane Sherron DeHart, *Women's America*, 5th edition (New York: Oxford University Press, 2000), 3–24

homes, and businesses.[30] At the same time they became "historians" and "journalists" who chronicled the progress of the war and its impact on their families and communities. Flora B. Avery was one of them. She highlighted community celebrations and the course of the war. In her July 8, 1863 entry she wrote, "As I am returning just at dusk the [citizens] begin to manifest their joy by the firing of guns and the ringing of bells and in various other ways for the war news still continues good and their enthusiasm breaks forth in noise and mirth. But alas! It brings my loneliness more forcefully to mind and speaks in too strong terms of the frightful cost."[31] Avery also observed the military's movement in her area and described their age and appearance.[32] She also was a keen observer of political issues surrounding the war at home and noted that there were "great riots" in Troy and New York on July 15, 1863.[33] Mary Peck recounted in great detail the jubilation that her townspeople expressed upon learning that General Lee had surrendered at Appomattox and suggested that gender tempered her response.[34]

Flora Avery provided another example of women's contributions on the home front. Avery made clothing, farmed, and provided aid to the indigent members of her community. She also prepared meals for the soldiers who were traveling through her community en route to the battlefields and noted the flag-waving and cheers that accompanied them.[35] Avery and her neighbors dried or pickled fruits and vegetables to send to the war front for the soldiers.[36] Making flags

---

[30] Francis Barnes even suggested that the war may have altered the relationship between spouses forever. Ibid., January 1, 1864, SC20332, Folder 5.

[31] Flora B. Avery Diary, July 8, 1863. Salisbury Center, Herkimer County, SC 18940, Manuscript Collection, New York State Library.

[32] Monday, April 13, 1863. "There was a brigade of soldiers passed today from Michigan. . . . They were fine looking—very clean and fresh looking. I should take them for new recruits—One little drummer boy I noticed that did not look as if he could be over 12 years of age. Alas! How melancholy."

[33] Ibid., July 15, 1863.

[34] "The old church bell in Castleton sent forth its many peals at intervals through the day and evening. . . . Then the bell at Orleans began to peal. I heard the canons at Canandaigua—Clifton—Phelps. I felt as if I must fly to hear the glorious sound for I knew they must be glorious! Bradley came . . . to tell Mr. B. [the news]. And the way they took off their caps and rent the air with their cheers! It seemed as I must join them—but I am a woman so I only said Thank God—and went in the house—& cried. . . ." Mary Peck to Henry Peck, April 12, 1865, SC 19406, MSC New York State Library.

[35] Flora B. Avery Diary, March 31, 1863.

[36] Flora B. Avery Diary, November 25, 1863.

allowed women to take their domestic skills into the public world of politics. In April 1861, R. W. Murphy observed that his wife Anne and the women of Burnt Hills were making a twenty-by-twenty-five-foot flag for a mass rally that would send men off to battle. He noted, "We cannot permit the Southern Seceders to have it all their own way and the Ladies are as warm in the cause and are all of them for *Union. The Union of the States! And the good of their country.*" [37] Socialite Eliza Woolsey presented the 16th New York regiment with a stand of state and national colors, made by Tiffany and Company, when it left Albany for Washington.[38] Some women expressed their support for the Union cause by wearing on Broadway that "fearful object of contemplation, 'a Union bonnet' composed of alternate layers of red, white, and blue, with streaming ribbons."[39]

Prominent socialite Jane Newton Woolsey of New York City, whose family had been Virginia plantation owners for generations, was a staunch abolitionist and avowed Unionist. She made her home at 8 Breevoort Place available to promote the cause. For months, bandage rolling was "the family fancywork, and other festivities really ceased." [40] Her home became a headquarters for the Union military and the new home to the campaign printing office. Some women were concerned about the quality of life of military men, including their educational needs. Elida B. Rumsey established a free library for soldiers in Judiciary Square in Washington on land that Congress had donated.[41]

Other groups of women organized to enhance their ability to make contributions to the war. New York women joined the U.S. Sanitary Commission, an organization that was dedicated to providing comfort for the military personnel; they made 26,000 quilts and sent them to the soldiers on the battlefield.[42] This was only one of many women's organizations that supported soldiers on the battlefield and their fam-

---

[37] R. W. Murphy Diary, Manuscripts 18464, New York State Library.
[38] Sylvia Dannett, *Noble Women of the North* (New York: Thomas Yoseloff, 1959), 76.
[39] Ibid., 45.
[40] Ibid., 30.
[41] Mary A. Gardner Holland, *Our Army Nurses* (Boston: Wilkins and Company, 1895), 67.
[42] See Judith Ann Giesberg, *Civil War Sisterhood* (Boston: Northeastern University Press, 2000).

ilies at home. Through their fundraising activities, women's groups raised huge amounts of money to support soldiers and the Union war effort. The Albany Army Relief Bazaar featured Professor Charles Doring and his band in a concert that performed classical and contemporary music to benefit the sick and wounded soldiers of the Union.[43] The Ladies Soldiers' Relief Society presented "dramatic entertainment" by Miss Mary C. Hathaway of the Parker Collegiate Institute of Brooklyn. This school reputedly was the most celebrated literary and scientific female institution in the country.[44] So while they raised money for the Union cause, they also were able to provide a forum for the artistic talents of women.

The war allowed women to play a more public role in other areas as well. It especially expanded the range of job opportunities for them and moved them out of the home and the domestic sphere. Nursing previously had fallen within the privatized labor sector. The large numbers of wounded and sick soldiers returning from the battlefield necessitated the creation of a profession and institutions to serve these veterans. Dorothea Dix devoted herself to hospital work. As superintendent of nurses she controlled all appointments and assignments.[45] All seven daughters of Jane Newton Woolsey became nurses in the war. Georgeanna Woolsey of New York City described the training of Civil War nurses in New York: "The Women's Relief Association organized a nursing staff for the army, selected 100 women and sent them to various New York City hospitals for training. The United States Sanitary Commission sought recognition for their contributions from the War Department with the pay of privates. They were sent to the army hospitals on requisitions from Dorothea Dix and others, 'as needed.' "[46] Georgeanna Woolsey and her sister Eliza Howland were among the first trainees and after they completed their education they went to war with Eliza's husband Joe, serving in Washington, D.C.[47] Nursing the sick and wounded military

---

[43] Broadsides 41, New York State Library.

[44] Dansville Ladies Soldier Relief Society, July 14, 1864, Broadside 1656, Manuscripts, New York State Library.

[45] Holland, *Our Army Nurses*, 33. See also Susie King Taylor, *Reminiscences of My Life in Camp* (New York: Arno Press and *The New York Times*, 1968), 42–43.

[46] Dannett, *Noble Women*, 63–64.

[47] Ibid., 74.

personnel provided opportunity for many young women to be independent, for they supported themselves and later some even received pensions for their military service.[48]

Still other women waged war, or acted as spies in defiance of the gender expectations of the day. Sarah Rosetta Wakeman and Harriet Tubman were two of the estimated 400 women who joined the Union and Confederate armed forces, most of them early in the war, when physical examinations for new recruits were not yet stringent. Wakeman, alias Private Lyons Wakeman, enlisted in the 153rd New York Volunteers in October 1862. She performed her duties diligently until she died in the federal army hospital in New Orleans on June 19, 1864.[49] While her military career places her among a small number of pioneering women, little is known about Wakeman's political views. Nor do we know why she did not reveal her gender to the medical staff at the military hospital. Did she believe that women would be condemned as a result of her activities, or did she fear the repercussions of being discovered as a female patient in an all-male establishment?

With a letter from Governor John A. Andrew of Massachusetts, Harriet Tubman reported on March 31, 1862 to General David Hunter at Hilton Head, S.C., where she worked effectively in the Union army as a cook, nurse, and spy. But Harriet Tubman also earned distinction as the only American woman to plan and execute a military expedition. In 1863, as an assistant to Colonel James Montgomery, she led a raid up the Combahee River from Port Royal, S.C., and destroyed many plantations that had provided provisions for Confederate troops. Known as the "Moses" of her people, in the process she freed some 800 slaves. In the spring and summer of 1865 Tubman worked briefly at a freedmen's hospital in Fortress Monroe, Virginia. Following her death from pneumonia in March 1913 she was honored with a full military funeral. She is buried in Fort Hill, Auburn, New York.[50]

---

[48] See, e.g., Lisa Y. King, "In Search of Women of African Descent Who Served in the Civil War Union Navy," *The Journal of Negro History* 83, #4 (Fall 1998) 307–308.

[49] Civil War Muster roll abstracts New York State Volunteers, United States Sharpshooters, and United States Colored Troops (ca. 1861–1900), roll 247, box 259, 153rd Infantry.

[50] Earl Conrad, *Harriet Tubman* (Washington, DC: Associated Publishers, 1943), 160–168; "Campaign on the Combahee", 169–178; 224. Also, see Sarah Bradford, *Harriet Tubman* (New York: Corinth, 1886).

Black women also saw service in the navy. Many were nurses, cooks, or domestics, while others donned male apparel and served alongside their husbands and other male relatives.[51] Still others, like Sojourner Truth, received appointments from the National Freedmen's Relief Association and became counselors to newly emancipated slaves. They taught them the skills that they would need to live and work in a free economy.[52] These women all made enormous contributions to the war effort. Simultaneously, they enhanced their skills in the area of public speaking and negotiations. Beyond that, they improved their ability to achieve economic self-sufficiency.

It took extraordinary courage for African Americans, regardless of their gender, to fight in the Civil War, for at the outset they faced discrimination in wages, work assignments, and treatment. They often were denied the status of prisoner of war when captured, and even risked the possibility of being sold into slavery. Further, the question of womanhood for African Americans was highly contested. From their arrival in the seventeenth century, black women were put to tasks that no white woman was expected to perform. They were not accorded the status of mother or citizen; hence, the republican mother ideology eluded them. Black women had been relegated to what Patricia Hill Collins describes as the controlling images of "Jezebel, Sapphire and Mammy."[53] Indeed, in 1851 Sojourner Truth deconstructed the meaning of womanhood to include women's strength, as well as the weaknesses that resulted from poverty or forced dependency, when she asked an Ohio audience, "Aren't I a Woman?" Nevertheless, black womanhood too often was violated. Some contended that black women's emotional make-up differed from that of white women. One observer commented that Irish women "are incensed when they think they are to be deprived of the companionship of their husbands [who were being drafted to free blacks], while no such sad catastrophe is likely to befall the nagur

---

[51] Lisa Y. King, "In Search of Women . . . ," 302–310.

[52] Olive Gilbert, *Sojourner Truth: Narrative and Book of Life* (Chicago: Johnson Publishing Company, reprinted 1970), 139; Carleton Mabee, *Sojourner Truth* (New York: New York University Press, 1993); Nell Irvin Painter, *Sojourner Truth: A Life, a Symbol* (New York: Norton, 1996). See also Taylor, *Reminiscences*, 21.

[53] Patricia Hill Collins, *Black Feminist Thought* (New York: Routledge, 1991), 67–90. For an expanded definition of black womanhood, see, Collins, *Black Feminist Thought*, 2nd edition (New York: Routledge, 2000), 69–96.

women."[54] Even Union soldiers marching through the South raped black women with virtual impunity.[55] So while military necessity had expanded the definition of womanhood for white women and black men, the struggle to achieve womanhood and respectability for African American women would remain an uphill battle and one that the National Association of Colored Women's Clubs would wage at the end of the nineteenth century and well into the twentieth.[56] So what's gender got to do with it? Men and women, white and black, were involved in every aspect of the war on the battlefield as well as on the home front. Men and women, regardless of their race, used the war to mediate the ideals of American democracy and directly linked the successful waging of the war to the extension of freedom. Black men gained freedom from slavery and the right to wage war, which ultimately resulted in their becoming enfranchised citizens—hence, men—but not until the ratification of the Fifteenth Amendment to the Constitution in 1870.[57] White women were em-

[54] Jacob C. White to Joseph C. Burstill, August 19, 1862, in Quarles, 183.

[55] The elderly Eliza Handy reported that the Union soldiers who passed her South Carolina home were "a bad lot [that] disgrace Mr. Lincoln" and insult black and white women. At Haine's Bluff, Mississippi, a white Union Army cavalryman raped "a grandmother in the presence of her grandchildren." White soldiers raped two Fortress Monroe, Virginia, women. Another woman was raped "after a desperate struggle" in the presence of "father and grandfather." A Natchez black wrote the *Christian Recorder* that husbands and fathers had witnessed the forcible violation of the virtue of their wives and daughters by white [Union] guards and soldiers." Blacks sought redress. Richmond blacks gathered in the Second African Baptist Church to petition the military authorities because Union Army soldiers were "gobbling . . . the most likely looking negro women" and placing them in the New Market Jail where some were "robbed and ravished at the will of the guards." They asked for protection or "the privilege of protecting themselves." Some black soldiers actually went AWOL to return home to protect their women from such outrages and remained there until the military assured them that their families would be safe. See Herbert G. Gutman, *The Black Family in Slavery and Freedom* (New York: Random House, 1976), 386–88. Chapter nine, "Let Not Man Put Asunder," offers detailed accounts of the sexual exploitation of African-American women by Union soldiers and the response of their community to such crimes (363–431).

[56] Darlene Clark Hine, "Rape and the Inner Lives of African-American Women," *Signs* 14 (1989) 912–920; Shaw, Stephanie J., *What a Woman Ought to Be and to Do* (Chicago: University of Chicago Press, 1996). See also Deborah Gray White, *Too Heavy a Load* (New York: W. W. Norton, 1999) and Lillian S. Williams, ed., *The Records of the National Association of Colored Women's Clubs, 1895–1990,* "Introduction," Volume I (Bethesda, Maryland: University Publications of America, 1993).

[57] William Seraille, "The Civil War's Impact on Race Relations in New York State, 1865–1875," *Afro-Americans in New York Life and History* 25 (January 2001), 57–89.

powered and began an aggressive campaign to get the vote. Black and white women experienced expanded job opportunities and greater access to the public sector and for some perhaps greater independence as a result of the Civil War. For unprecedented numbers of African-American women the war provided an opportunity to work in a free labor market for the first time. Their inclusion into the category of American woman, however, remained on contested ground. By successfully waging the Civil War, Northern white men were assured that their freedom was certain and that bondage would not be an element that could undermine that freedom.

4

In the Shadow of American Indian Removal: The Iroquois in the Civil War

Laurence M. Hauptman

SOME 20,000 AMERICAN INDIANS served in the Civil War. They contributed to Union and Confederate causes on both land and sea, as "grunts" in the trenches, and even as commissioned and noncommissioned officers. From Virginia to Indian Territory, Native Americans found themselves swept up into a war not of their choosing. The Iroquois Indians—the Mohawks, Oneidas, Onondagas, Cayugas, Senecas, and Tuscaroras—were no different in that regard. Approximately 600 Iroquois—nearly 10 percent of the population of their reservations in New York, Wisconsin, and Indian Territory—served the Union during the Civil War.[1]

In recent years, historians James M. McPherson and Earl J. Hess have tried to explain why Civil War soldiers "fought like 'bulldogs' " (McPherson's own words) and were more willing to take such heavy casualties, battle after battle, than in later wars.[2] Both historians attempt to counter the writings of Gerald F. Linderman, who had insisted that the harrowing combat experiences of Civil War soldiers

---

[1] See Laurence M. Hauptman, *The Iroquois in the Civil War* (Syracuse: Syracuse University Press, 1993); Hauptman, *Between Two Fires: American Indians in the Civil War* (New York: Simon & Schuster, 1995), chapter 9; and Hauptman, ed., *A Seneca Sergeant in the Union Army: The Civil War Letters of Sergeant Isaac Newton Parker, 1861–1865* (Shippensburg, Pa.: Burd Street Press/White Mane Publishing, 1995).

[2] James M. McPherson, *For Cause and Comrades: Why Men Fought in the Civil War* (New York: Oxford University Press, 1997), 5–13; and Earl J. Hess, *The Union Soldier in Battle: Enduring the Ordeal of Combat* (Lawrence, Kansas: University Press of Kansas, 1997), 192–98.

resulted in the abandonment of idealism; to Linderman, by the last years of the conflict, Civil War soldiers fought merely to survive, not for a cause or for honor.[3] McPherson maintained that these soldiers did not generally fight for the money, nor simply because of the coercive structure of the military of the North and South. They fought largely for duty, honor, and the pursuit of liberty, and for the welfare of their comrades-in-arms. Wartime volunteers held firm to their values from civilian life, remaining "rooted in the homes and communities" from which they sprang.[4]

By focusing solely on Union soldiers, Hess, countering Linderman, has rejected what he labels the "modernist perspective," insisting that the Civil War was a nineteenth-century conflict far different from later wars.[5] With World War I, the "shock of modern warfare, with its advanced technology and its tendency to make targets of civilian populations, demanded a new attitude toward warfare that inevitably condemned it."[6] In contrast, the Civil War was a domestic tragedy, not a foreign conflict that "inspired deep passions and moral fervor." Hess argued that Americans of the Civil War era generally placed more emphasis on ideology, patriotism, religion, and civic virtue than did twentieth-century soldiers. In conclusion, Hess asserted:

> The Northern soldier fought a traditional war in all respects, but particularly in his mind. The mental and emotional field of battle was the most old-fashioned of all. He looked to the past for inspiration and guides to his own action. Thus, the example of the Founding Fathers and the ideology they created came into play more prominently than modern attitudes that would be typical of a future age.[7]

What explains the significant presence of so many American Indians in the Civil War? Does the recent historiography of Civil War combat provide answers? I must conclude that much of the recent writings on the subject have little relevance to the American Indian experience. American Indians felt much more patriotic to their own nations than to the Stars and Stripes or to the Stars and Bars. Main-

---

[3] Gerald F. Linderman, *Embattled Courage: The Experience of Combat in the American Civil War* (New York: Macmillan, 1987), 2, 240.

[4] McPherson, *For Cause and Comrades*, 5–13.

[5] Hess, *The Union Soldier in Battle*, ix–x, 197–98.

[6] Ibid., 197.

[7] Ibid., 197–98.

taining homeland was and remains a constant in Indian country. Nearly all Indians who participated in the war—North, South, and trans-Mississippi West—hoped to preserve themselves and their communities from further land loss and removal. Indeed, Indian removal policies were the backdrop to American Indian involvement in the war. All American Indians were increasingly surrounded and dependent on their white neighbors and caught between two fires. Faced with a precarious existence, American Indians in all three regions saw military involvement as their only chance, the last desperate hope of securing their land base.

The most famous of the Iroquois units in the Civil War from New York State was D Company of the 132d New York Volunteer Infantry. D Company was popularly referred to as the Tuscarora Company, because part of the unit was recruited by Lieutenant Cornelius C. Cusick, a Tuscarora Indian. In reality, the company was largely composed of German immigrants, mostly artisans and merchants recruited in Brooklyn, and twenty-five Iroquois farmers from western New York. The Iroquois Indians were mostly Senecas from Allegany, Cattaraugus, Cornplanter, and Tonawanda Indian Reservations with a sprinkling of Cayugas, Onondagas, Oneidas, and Tuscaroras. Iroquois recruits in the 132d New York Volunteer Infantry ranged in age from eighteen to thirty-eight, averaging approximately twenty-six years. The recruits had been born in the 1830s and early 1840s, an especially traumatic time in Iroquois history.[8] The Treaty of Buffalo Creek of 1838 was at the center of Iroquois life, a fact that was not lost on youngsters growing up in reservation households or listening to elders in council meetings. The treaty would have vast consequences for Iroquoian life in New York, Wisconsin, Indian Territory, and Canada.

The Treaty of Buffalo Creek, concluded between tribesmen in New York and the federal government, resulted in the permanent loss of the Senecas' Buffalo Creek Reservation, the center of Iroquois traditional life after the American Revolution. The treaty, affecting all Six Nations and the Stockbridge-Munsees, led to the removal of many Indians from the state. The treaty was fraudulently consummated through bribery, forgery, the use of alcohol, and other nefarious methods. In it the Senecas ceded all their remaining New York

---

[8] Hauptman, *The Iroquois in the Civil War*, 25–45.

lands to the Ogden Land Company and relinquished their rights to Indian lands in Wisconsin purchased for them by the United States. In return, the Indians accepted a 1,824,000-acre reservation in Kansas set aside by the federal government for all the six Iroquois nations as well as the Stockbridge-Munsee. The Indian nations had to occupy these Kansas lands within five years or forfeit them. For their 102,069 acres in New York, the Indians were to receive $202,000, $100,000 to be invested in safe stocks by the president of the United States; the income earned was to be returned to the Indians. The United States was also to provide a modest sum to facilitate removal, establish schools, and purchase farm equipment and livestock for the Indians' use.[9]

The treaty had other far-reaching effects. Many Indians died of cholera, exposure, or starvation en route to or in Indian Territory. In addition, the bitter infighting over tribal policies after the treaty's consummation eventually led to the creation of a new political entity, the Seneca Nation of Indians, in 1848. Moreover, the treaty led to a Quaker-directed campaign to restore the Indian land base in New York and resulted in the United States Senate's ratification of a "compromise treaty" in 1842. The Senecas regained the Allegany and Cattaraugus but not the Buffalo Creek and Tonawanda reservations. Only in 1856 was the Tonawanda Band of Senecas finally allowed to purchase a small part of its reservation back from the Ogden Land Company. This land purchase as well as the confirmation of federal reservation status was acknowledged by the United States and the Tonawanda Band of Senecas in a treaty concluded the following year. American Indian claims under the 1838 treaty were not settled until the 1890s in a major United States Court of Claims award. Thus the Buffalo Creek Treaty was the basis of much of federal-Iroquois relations throughout the nineteenth century.[10]

Well after the 1838 treaty, the Iroquois faced efforts to remove

---

[9] For the Treaty of Buffalo Creek, see Charles J. Kappler, comp., *Indian Affairs: Laws and Treaties* (Washington, DC: U.S. Government Printing Office, 1903–1941), 2: 502–16; reprinted in one volume as *Indian Treaties, 1778–1883* (Mattituck, NY: Amereon House, 1972), 502–516. For the frauds, see Henry S. Manley, "Buying Buffalo from the Indians," *New York History* 28 (July 1947): 313–29.

[10] For a thorough analysis of Iroquois land loss under the Treaty of Buffalo Creek, see Laurence M. Hauptman, *Conspiracy of Interests: Iroquois Dispossession and the Rise of New York State* (Syracuse: Syracuse University Press, 1999), chapters 10–12.

them from their homeland. Philip E. Thomas, the prominent Baltimore Quaker philanthropist and advocate for the Seneca Indians, wrote George W. Manypenny, the commissioner of Indian Affairs, in June 1855, protesting the actions of "heartless" whites who were "determined to wrest from them [the Senecas] the land and drive them to destruction. Calling the Senecas a "cruelly wronged people," Thomas advocated federal intervention to protect the Indians. Despite this protest, the New York State comptroller in Albany the following year initiated tax foreclosure proceedings on 1,100 acres of the Cattaraugus Indian Reservation.[11]

Iroquois fears of being removed from their New York homeland continued unabated even after the formal Seneca ratification of the Tonawanda Treaty in 1857. Councilors of the Seneca Nation of Indians drew up a petition on June 2, 1858, insisting that the "council is strongly opposed to any commissioner being appointed on the part of the United States for the purpose of negotiating any treaty with Seneca Nation respecting any proposed sale of their lands in the State of New York or elsewhere." The petition, which was forwarded to President James Buchanan and the Bureau of Indian Affairs, revealed that certain persons were circulating "petitions among our peoples" asking for negotiations encouraging emigration "in order to draw off our people from their present condition."[12] At approximately the same time, Thomas further elaborated on the plan to rid New York of Iroquois Indians by "rapacious land sharks that are hovering about them." He added that these forces aimed to "find means to corrupt and secure the co-operation of certain unprincipled individuals among the Indians" to effect their removal to Kansas.[13] Thus the more important "impending crisis" for the Iroquois was not the approaching Civil War but the need to defend the Indian land base. Yet

[11] Philip E. Thomas to George W. Manypenny, June 6, 1855; Marcus H. Johnson to George Manypenny, Nov. 25, 1856, with attached notice of a sale of land for taxes, Oct. 10, 1856, signed by Harvey Baldwin, New York Agency Records, OIA, M234, MR588, RG75, National Archives [NA]; Nathaniel Starbuck to "Respected Friend," Mar. 12, 1856, and Philip E. Thomas to George T. Trimble, Amos Willetts, and William C. White, Nov. 20, 1856, Papers and Letters Relating to the Work of the Joint Indian Committee of Four Yearly Meetings, 1835–63, File 21, 1856–57, New York Yearly Meeting, Haviland Record Room, New York City.

[12] Petition of the Councilors of the Seneca Nation to the President of the United States, June 2, 1858, New York Agency Records, OIA, M234, MR589, RG75, NA.

[13] Fragment of a letter written by Philip E. Thomas, 1859 or 1859?, New York Agency, OIA, M234, MR589 (plate 0089), RG75, NA.

the secession crisis in 1860–1861 was not merely a curiosity to the Iroquois. They feared its implications and worried about the future of their land claims and its impact on the New York Indian Agency.[14] As Confederate artillery pieces were aimed at Fort Sumter during the secession crisis of 1860–1861, Washington officials discussed or made plans for continued Indian removals as an option to solve the so-called "Indian Problem." The United States Army, during the years of heaviest fighting during the Civil War, undertook campaigns of "pacification" against the Indians in the Great Lakes, Northwest, Plains, and Southwest. While the Confederate constitutional convention was meeting in February 1861 at Montgomery, Alabama, the United States Army was attempting to capture Cochise, the Apache leader. At the end of the Seven Days Battles on July 1, 1862, the United States Congress passed legislation authorizing the building of the Transcontinental Railroad. When it was completed seven years later, the link contributed to the disruption of traditional Plains Indian life, resulted in the extermination of bison herds, brought massive non-Indian population westward, increased Indian-white tension and conflicts, and led to reservation existence and overall Indian dependence. Less than two weeks before the Second Battle of Bull Run in August of the same year, the "Great Sioux Uprising" began in Minnesota.

While the Union army in March 1864 was undertaking an ambitious campaign up the Red River of Louisiana with the intention of capturing Shreveport and invading Confederate Texas, General James Carleton was ordering Kit Carson to force the Indians out of their citadel at Canyon de Chelly. Throughout 1864, eight thousand Navajos and Mescalero Apaches were removed and relocated, for a four-year stay, at a concentration camp, the Bosque Redondo, at Fort Sumner, New Mexico. Two weeks after Lincoln's re-election in November 1864, Colonel John Chivington and the troops of the 1st and 3rd Colorado Cavalry attacked a peaceful camp of mostly Cheyenne Indians along the Sand Creek, killing about 150 men, women, and children and mutilating their bodies.

To most Native Americans, including the Iroquois, almost all of whom were non-citizens, the Civil War was a foreign conflict, but

[14] Nicholson Parker to Ely S. Parker, May 17, 1860, Ely S. Parker MSS., American Philosophical Society [APS], Philadelphia.

one that inspired nonetheless a deep passion and moral fervor. They looked to the past, to their own separate Indian cultures, for inspiration, a past different from that of white soldiers. American Indian soldiers' idealism was inspired not by the Founding Fathers and the system they created, but by past chiefs and clan mothers who advocated community survival in the face of overwhelming land losses since the time of the Constitution, by individual factors necessitating their community's involvement in war, and, despite McPherson's claims, economic necessity resulting from their extreme poverty. To be sure, some Indian communities had by 1861 been integrated into the region that surrounded them, becoming dependent on the non-Indian world for economic and political survival. For some individual Indian soldiers, their recruitment in the Civil War was inspired by wanderlust and search for adventure. In other instances, it was also based on past alliances, treaty obligations, and earlier military experiences. As in olden days, participation in war validated tribal leadership and status within one's community. Moreover, Native Americans had their own views about slavery, leading at times to internal disputes and civil wars, as some Indians—not the Iroquois—were slaveholders and others were opposed to the "peculiar institution." Frequently, the reasons for volunteering were simply the result of persuasive and well-respected community leaders who were committed to joining the war effort of North or South. Most of all, it was their tenuous existence in both the North and South that brought so many of the Indian nations to the Confederate or Union sides in 1861. They were dependent peoples as a result of American wars of conquest, treaties, or economic, political, social, and religious changes introduced by the "Long Knives." From Connecticut to Indian Territory, they sought the "warpath" because it seemed imperative for their own economic and/or their Indian community's survival.

Union armies were significantly affected by the presence of Iroquois Indian troops. At Vicksburg, Indians in the 14th Wisconsin, mostly Oneidas, an Iroquoian community who had been removed west from 1820 to 1838, camouflaged themselves with leaves, crawled on their bellies to get into position, and then silenced the "rebel cannon in front [of our position] almost entirely."[15] A year

---

[15] Joseph Stockton Diary quoted in Richard Wheeler, *The Siege of Vicksburg* (1978 paperback reprint, New York: Harper Perennial, 1991), 202.

later, Seneca soldiers of the 14th New York Heavy Artillery replicated the Wisconsin Indians' action by camouflaging themselves and capturing a nest of rebel snipers at the Battle of Spotsylvania. Despite the heroism of these soldiers, the Northern newspaper account portrayed their actions in stereotypical fashion. One of the Senecas, Oliver Silverheels, was described by the *New York Herald* as being just like one of James Fenimore Cooper's Indians, "rivaling the 'deviltry' of any of the Leatherstocking redskins." Newspapers well after the war recounted the famous capture in similar ways. The *Warren Mail* later added Tonto-like dialogue to Silverheels's actions: "You go heap straight[,] me no shoot; you look back[,] me kill you. . . . Drop gun, come down, or me shoot you dead. Me no tell again."[16]

American Indians also had an important impact on Union regimental life. According to one Civil War veteran, Dudley Beekman of New York City, "As near as I can remember there were some 25 Indians in Co. D [132d New York Volunteer Infantry] all of this state and all could talk *american* for I was often with them and considered them pretty good fellows[.] it was these same indians that taught me to swim."[17] Especially noteworthy were the Oneida Indians of the 14th Wisconsin. These Oneidas' enlistment came directly out of economic necessity. Their enlistments came late—from December 1863 to the early months of 1864. M. M. Davis, the federal Indian agent at Green Bay, later wrote that they joined of "their own free will. They have received Government and local bounties and I have no doubt that they are much better provided for in the service than they have ever been heretofore. The families of these enlisted men are also much better off than heretofore. They already received large bounties and they receive $5 per month from the state."[18] They were resourceful in securing food and, even more, in preparing it. Private Elisha Stockwell described how one of the F Company Indians, armed with his Belgian rifle, went squirrel shooting and came back to camp "with all the squirrels he could handily carry, all shot in the

---

[16] James C. Fitzpatrick, "The Ninth Corps," *New York Herald*, June 30, 1864; "Chief Silverheels Capture," *Warren [Pa.] Mail*, Aug. 23, 1887.

[17] Dudley A. Beekman to Col. Hugh Hastings, March 21, 1897, Grand Army of the Republic MSS., 132d New York State Volunteer Infantry, Package 14, New York State Library.

[18] M. M. Davis to W. P. Dole, May 31, 1864, Green Bay Agency Records, 1861–1864, OIA, M234, MR234, RG75, NA.

head." Squirrel soup, an Oneida and other Iroquois Indians' favorite, was a welcome substitute for stale hardtack.[19] Lieutenant James K. Newton of De Pere, commander of Company F, who lived adjacent to the Oneida Indian Reservation, made reference to a culinary delight "discovered" by his regiment's recruits:

> You would not believe how many ways we can cook our corn so as to have a variety. We have parched corn, boiled Do. mush, corn coffee etc. but the latest invention to make it go down good is to half parch it, and then grind it coarse like hominy and then boil it with a small piece of pork to season it. If you have to live on corn altogether, by reason of this war's continuing for a great length of time longer I advise you to cook it in the way I last mentioned.[20]

Parched hominy seasoned with salt pork is a typical Iroquois recipe, "Onon'daat." It has been described as an Indian dish since earliest European contact and is often referred to as sagamite, sapaen, or suppawn.[21]

Unlike many of their Iroquoian kin in Wisconsin, who were lured largely by significant bounty payments late in the war, Indians in New York attempted to join the Union war effort from the beginning. Despite the claims of their white officers, the reason for Iroquois military service in the Civil War does not appear to be simple patriotism to the Constitution or to the flag of the United States, so evident in the North in 1861. Even though they referred to the South's "Devilism and Rebelism" in letters, they looked somewhat askance at white officers who rallied the troops solely on the basis of patriotic duty. Yet, like other Northerners, they perceived the attack on Fort Sumter, the secession, and the "War of the Rebellion" as an affront to them.[22]

---

[19] Elisha Stockwell, Jr., *Private Elisha Stockwell, Jr., Sees the Civil War*, Byron R. Abernethy, ed. (Norman, OK: University of Oklahoma Press, 1958), 32–33, 74–75, 79–80, 88–89.

[20] James K. Newton, *A Wisconsin Boy in Dixie: The Selected Letters of James K. Newton*, Stephen E. Ambrose, ed. (Madison: University of Wisconsin Press, 1961), 138–39.

[21] Arthur C. Parker, *Parker on the Iroquois*, William N. Fenton, ed. (Syracuse: Syracuse University Press, 1968), 73–74; Recipe of Amelia Williams (Tuscarora) in Marlene Johnson, comp., *Iroquois Cookbook*, 2nd ed. (Tonawanda Indian Reservation: Peter Doctor Memorial Indian Fellowship Foundation, 1989), 8.

[22] Isaac Newton Parker to Sara Jemison Parker, Aug. 17, 1862, Isaac Newton Parker MSS., Buffalo & Erie County Historical Society [BECHS], Buffalo.

What appears to whites as simply acculturative forces at work—in this case enlistment in a white man's war—was and is still viewed by the Iroquois as acceptable and logical Indian behavior. Many Iroquois people in New York do not choose to vote in off-reservation local, state, and national elections, choosing instead to participate in tribal referenda. Yet this separation does not prevent them from opening pow-wows with an American flag ceremony and a color guard to honor Indian and non-Indian veterans of past wars, including those who fought on the side of white men. However strange they seem to the dominant white society, these actions, which also include valued memberships in the Veterans of Foreign Wars and the American Legion posts in nearly every Iroquois community, are all part of the complex that makes up Indian identity.[23]

Military service was and still is an honored profession in Iroquois ranks. In protesting that Iroquois in New York were first denied entrance into military service in 1861, Cayuga spokesman and physician Peter Wilson pointed this fact out. "Farmer's Brother was my Great Grandfather, Young King my Grandfather and he was a personal friend of General Porter. He was wounded in the leg at the skirmish at Black Rock. For his bravery and services he was [honored?] by a special act of Congress—I think in 1815. My father Col. Reuben James was a private during the War of 1812 and was present at the Battle of Chippawa, where his brother was killed."[24]

Despite religious proscriptions set in the early nineteenth century by the prophet Handsome Lake against entering white men's wars, Iroquois warrior-soldiers joined and excelled during this and later wars. Moreover, validation of tribal leadership through war, which had been an important part of life in the seventeenth and eighteenth centuries, was still meaningful to Iroquois youth in mid-nineteenth-

---

[23] Today, nearly every Iroquois community has an active veterans' organization which has an important impact on the cultural, political, and social life of each reservation. The Iroquois were active in the GAR. See Hauptman, *The Iroquois in the Civil War*, photograph opposite p. 101. Col. T.S. Strohecker to My Dear Comrade (Willett Pierce), postcard reminder of "annual reunion of the 57th Regiment, Pennsylvania Veteran Volunteer Infantry, Oct. 17, 1901." Civil War Collection, Seneca-Iroquois National Museum, Salamanca, N.Y. Interview of George Heron, July 3, 1990, Allegany Indian Reservation. Mr. Heron, former president of the Seneca Nation and a highly decorated veteran of World War II, remembered the GAR Indian veterans' funerals, specifically of Philip Fatty, in the 1920s.

[24] Peter Wilson to General Scroggs, Nov. 11, 1861, Letters Concerning Indian Volunteers, Wilkeson Family MSS., Box 11, BECHS.

century America. As in the case of Peter Wilson, many fathers and grandfathers of Civil War volunteers had served proudly in the colonial wars, the American Revolution, and the War of 1812.[25] Some, such as Cornelius C. Cusick and Ely S. and Isaac Newton Parker, were members of families with extensive military traditions and logically sought out service.

In an earlier era, ambitious individuals with talent, such as Cusick and the Parkers, were free to form war parties. War, then and now, had a key status function. The historian Barbara Graymont has noted that "war gave rise to a prominence of men who achieved their fame by ability rather than inheritance. . . . Prestigious titles were thus restricted to certain reigning families." Graymont added, "An ordinary man, however, might rise to note by merit alone if he had the proven qualities of courage and shrewdness required of a warrior." In 1776, 1812, 1861, 1898, 1917, 1941, 1950, 1965, and 1991, talented individuals could thus take their place in the community by gaining recognition and prestige on the warpath. A warrior, as well as other men of high ability, could become a pine tree chief, an elective office that was not hereditary as was that of sachem. They could serve as advisers to the sachems or might even become "far more noteworthy than sachems."[26] Although much had changed since the American Revolution, war served as a way to move up in the ranks of society well into the nineteenth century. Samuel George, the noted Onondaga runner and hero of the War of 1812, rose in prominence through military service, as did LaFort, Young King, Farmer's Brother, and others. By the time of the Civil War, Chief George of the Onondagas had become the "Great Wolf," the consensus builder, keeper of the wampum, and spokesman for the Iroquois Confederacy.[27]

American Indians in the Union Army came from a separate cul-

---

[25] See Barbara Graymont, *The Iroquois in the American Revolution* (Syracuse: Syracuse University Press, 1973); Carl Benn, *The Iroquois in the War of 1812* (Toronto: Toronto University Press, 1998).

[26] Graymont, *The Iroquois in the American Revolution*, 20–23. The scholarly literature on Iroquois literature is extensive. Besides Graymont and Benn, see Anthony F. C. Wallace, *The Death and Rebirth of the Seneca* (New York: Knopf, 1970), 30–50; Daniel Richter, "War and Culture: The Iroquois Experience," *William and Mary Quarterly*, 3d ser., no. 4 (1983): 537–44.

[27] See, for example, Laurence M. Hauptman, "Samuel George (1795–1873): A Study of Onondaga Conservatism," *New York History* 70 (Jan. 1989): 4–22.

tural universe. They went to war as representatives from Indian communities, faced combat influenced by the ethos of warrior existence,
performed Indian rituals in the face of death, and returned home
to cleansing ceremonies to return them to the normality of Indian
existence. While they bonded with their non-Indian comrades in
their efforts to survive, most Indians in the Union army joined in
clusters, often volunteering on the same day or returning home with
their Indian neighbors. For example, seven of twenty-five Iroquois
from the Cattaraugus Indian Reservation enlisted on the same day:
May 4, 1862.[28]

Ely Parker's experience at the Battle of Chattanooga, described in
his letters at the American Philosophical Society in Philadelphia, are
the fullest portrayal of an Iroquois Indian in combat for the Union
during the Civil War. Even as a highly acculturated Indian, Parker
adds further proof to my point about American Indians in combat,
namely, that they brought the values and social norms of their own
Indian communities, not necessarily those of the United States, into
combat. Parker's way of dealing with the horrors of Civil War battle
was directly tied to the cultural traditions of his Seneca people, and
do not necessarily fit entirely with McPherson's or Hess's generaliza-
tions or Linderman's conclusions.

Historians have long been intrigued by the Civil War career of Ely
S. Parker, the first Native American to serve as Commissioner of
Indian Affairs. After receiving a commission in the Union army in
May 1863, Parker served as assistant adjutant general, division engineer, and, most importantly, General Ulysses S. Grant's military secretary. By the end of the war, he had been promoted to brigadier
general and served as Grant's scribe, drawing up the articles of surrender which General Robert E. Lee signed on April 9, 1865, at
Appomattox Court House, Virginia.[29]

---

[28] Hauptman, *The Iroquois in the Civil War*, 28–31.

[29] There are two major biographies of Ely S. Parker: William Armstrong, *Warrior
in Two Camps: Ely S. Parker, Union General and Seneca Chief* (Syracuse, 1978);
and Arthur C. Parker, *The Life of General S. Parker, Last Grand Sachem of the
Iroquois and General Grant's Military Secretary*. Buffalo Historical Society *Publications*, XXIII (Buffalo, 1919). See also Elisabeth Tooker, "Ely S. Parker: Seneca, ca.
1828–1895." In: *American Indian Intellectuals*, Margot Liberty, ed. (St. Paul, Minn.,
1978), 15–30; Henry G. Waltmann, "Ely Samuel Parker (1869–1871)." In: *The Com-
missioners of Indian Affairs, 1824–1877*, Robert Kvasnicka and Herman Viola, Eds.
(Lincoln, Neb., 1979), 123–34; and William S. McFeeley, *Grant: A Biography* (New

Parker was no ordinary man. His grandfather Jemmy Johnson was a nephew of the celebrated Seneca orator Red Jacket and was the leading disciple of the great Seneca prophet Handsome Lake, who was also in Parker's lineage. Hence, Parker's blood lines tied him to both political and religious leadership and separated him from other Senecas, and his battlefield letters at Chattanooga reflect that point. Hence, it was no coincidence that the Parkers' two-story homestead at the Tonawanda Reservation during the Jacksonian–Van Buren era became the center of political activity against the fraudulent Treaty of Buffalo Creek of 1838, which dispossessed his people, and that Parker devoted more than a decade of his life to that effort.[30] Indeed, Parker's struggle to regain his people's lands taken during the age of Indian removal largely influenced his perceptions and writings even during the Battle of Chattanooga in November 1863, his first experience in combat.

On November 18, 1863, Parker, with the exuberance of first combat, wrote a revealing letter to his brother Nicholson from Grant's headquarters near Chattanooga, an area which he referred to as a "God forsaken country." Accurately predicting a major battle, Parker insisted that General Braxton Bragg's Confederates, the "flower and bulk of the Southern Army," would be wise to flee before the Union forces thrashed them and pushed them out of the region. He added that the enemy was "here within speaking distance in one front." Graphically describing the circumstances, the Seneca officer suggested that Nicholson and others in the North "who are out of the reach of the noise, excitement, and hardships" of army life "cannot begin to realize what war is." According to Parker, war was two ar-

York, 1981; New York: W. W. Norton paperback edition, 1982), 88, 146, 160, 286, 305–318. For Parker's role at Appomattox, see: "General Ely S. Parker's Narrative" [of General Lee's Surrender at Appomattox], Ulysses S. Grant MSS., Series 8, Box 2, Library of Congress, Manuscript Division, Washington, DC; Sylvanus Cadwalader, *Three Years with Grant*, Benjamin P. Thomas, ed. (New York: Alfred A. Knopf, 1956), 323; Horace Parker, *Campaigning with Grant* (New York: Century, 1897); paperback reprint New York: Da Capo, 1986), 33–34, 200, 207–208, 476–81; and John Y. Simon, *The Papers of Ulysses S. Grant* (Carbondale, IL: Southern Illinois University, 1979), XIV: 361, 374–78.

[30] Armstrong, *Warrior in Two Camps*, 1–60; Parker, *The Life of General Ely S. Parker . . .*, 234–35. For Parker's efforts to overturn the treaty, see Ely S. Parker and Isaac Shanks [Seneca Delegates] to Commissioner of Indian Affairs William Medill, Jan. 20, 1848, Letters Received by the Office of Indian Affairs, 1824–1881, Records of the New York Agency, M324, Microfilm Reel 587, Record Group 75, NA.

mies face to face, whose "whole study and object is to destroy one another" with scouting parties, heavy cannonade, and deadly missiles scattering in every direction. He admitted that he was no longer afraid since he had been numbed by the entire experience and that he could go to "regular battle as calmly as I would go to my meal when hungry." Despite casual references to death, he specified his will and his intentions about the distribution of his property if he fell in battle. He indicated, however, that he had every plan "to come home and settle down once more upon my farm, and go to work as all honest men do."[31]

Parker also revealed that he had been seriously ill, which resulted in his losing thirty pounds; he added that he was now recovering on a diet of beef, bread, and coffee. His health was apparently not well served by his having been forced to sleep in exposed conditions. This illness was to plague Parker throughout the Battle of Chattanooga and for several months afterwards. At a time when his father's health was in decline, Parker regretfully indicated that he had no money to send home and that he was heavily in debt. In concluding his letter, he sent his regards to his family and to Asher and Laura Wright, the well-respected Presbyterian missionaries to the Senecas. Almost psychically, Parker added that he believed that a "great commotion is about to take place among these hills."[32]

Equally significant was Parker's letter to his sister Caroline, dated November 21. He first expressed his concerns about his father's failing health, the serious crop failures at Tonawanda, his own slow recovery from illness, the treacherous mountain battle terrain of the Cumberland Mountains, and the death of his trusted steed which he had foolishly lent to a fellow Union officer. Parker then warned that the "rebel army are south, east and west of us. In fact they almost surround us." He then drew a map of the city and the position of the federal troops, later suggesting that the "mountainous country and the summits of the mountains are almost inaccessible." According to the Seneca officer, Union and Confederate armies were in such proximity that, according to Parker, "our pickets can talk with the rebel pickets." As was true of the Union command during the war, Parker seriously underestimated the number of enemy troops, put-

---

[31] Ely S. Parker to Nicholson Parker, Nov. 18, 1863, Ely S. Parker MSS., APS.
[32] Ibid.

ting them at 60,000 strong. "They fire us every day with cannon from the top of Lookout Mountain which hangs over our city one-half mile above the plain we occupy." Union guns at Moccasin Point, 1,200 feet below the Confederate on the mountain, responded in kind, leading Parker to comment: "No day passes that the cannons are not engaged." Although the battle for Chattanooga did not formally begin until several days later, Parker estimated that 500 or 600 men had already been killed in the vicinity of the city.[33]

In the same letter, Parker then focused on the war's impact on the South as well as his own perceptions of the region and its peoples. He suggested that rural Southerners "do not live as well or as comfortable as the Tonawanda Indians," not really a surprise after three bloody years of conflict. He insisted that "the negroes, once slaves, of course are all with us and are our servants to pay." He then went on to describe the Southerners' round log country houses, mostly deserted at the time, claiming chauvinistically that "any Indian house is better and more comfortable and cleaner." Parker noted that prewar textiles manufactured in the North were no longer available and that Southern women were wearing "coarse homespun dresses very much like our old-fashioned flannel, usually called domestic flannel." The Seneca officer then bemoaned the fate of the South, while chiding Confederate leaders such as General Bragg, at every turn: "O Carrie! This is a most desolate country, and no human being can realize or comprehend the dreadful devastation and horrors created by war, until they have been in its track." The ruins of war were nearly everywhere. He added that just one hundred miles from Louisville, all you see are "lone chimneys standing where once may have been a fine mansion." To Parker, only one acre out of one hundred was still being cultivated in this region and weeds were dominating the landscape.[34]

As a man of chiefly lineage and Western education, Parker reflected some of the biases of men of his station as well as those of the age. In and around Chattanooga, the Seneca sachem found "only poor 'white trash' " who were "so poor that they can hardly speak the English language" and who have a "blind infatuation" for the

---

[33] Ely S. Parker to Caroline Parker Mountpleasant, Nov. 21, 1863, Ely S. Parker MSS., APS.
[34] Ibid.

Confederate cause. He observed that, in other areas of the South, blacks were now occupying great Southern mansions and had stripped these homes of their fine mahogany and rosewood furniture to furnish their own cabins. Fine dresses "that white ladies once be-decked themselves with, now hang shabbily upon the ungainly figure of some huge, dilapidated Negro wench," wrote Parker sadly, re-flecting both his own elitism based on his distinguished lineage as well as racist acculturated attitudes. Thus, Parker, a man of limited wealth who was frequently in debt, identified more with the white planter class of the South whose lifeways were being shattered by the American Civil War than either the lower white classes who com-posed much of the Confederate armies or the black freedman.[35]

In this respect, Parker's view matches one described by other Union soldiers. Historian Reid Mitchell has observed that Union sol-diers often viewed the South during the Civil War as a foreign coun-try full of cruelty, decadence, and savagery. In this "bizarre and hostile environment," soldiers found signs of extreme poverty and sloth as well as decaying houses, farms, and plantations. In this "unre-deemed" land, they witnessed "evidence" of an "inferior culture" all around them. Judged subjectively by these visitors' eyes, the South and its white inhabitants were found wanting. Nor were Southern blacks perceived any better. Union soldiers often judged them to be "exotic beings" as well as being "dirty, ignorant, superstitious and lazy." In this forbidding setting with its strange inhabitants, these soldiers had to endure some of the most intense fighting in American history. With anonymous corpses littering a myriad Civil War battle-fields, Union troops had to overcome their fears of becoming casual-ties by ignoring the "humanity of the men who died. Men became numb."[36]

Yet Parker's same letter of November 21 also reveals much about his own frame of reference, namely, that he was still Seneca-centered in his ways, even as death was all around him. Parker's keen interest in Native American history was also revealed in this same letter. Chattanooga, although a sixteenth-century Creek village, had long-established roots in Cherokee history. Cherokee Chief John Ross's

[35] Ibid.
[36] Reid Mitchell, *Civil War Soldiers: Their Expectations and Their Experiences* (New York: Viking Press, 1988), 25–26, 64–65, 90–92, 107.

boyhood home (1797–1808) was at the base of the northern end of the Lookout Mountain range at present-day Chattanooga. At the death of his mother, Ross moved to the Lookout Mountain Valley, in an area which became known as Rossville. Later, in 1838, five groups of Cherokees were removed westward from Ross's Landing in the Trail of Tears.[37] Parker reflected upon being in Cherokee Country. He informed his sister that we "are here in the ancient homes of the Cherokees, and our present quarters are only about 12 miles from John Ross' old home." To Parker, a Seneca Indian who had resisted emigration west under the Treaty of Buffalo Creek and who had fought so fervently to win back the Tonawanda lands, Ross, the head of the Cherokee anti-removal party, was a living legend and his homestead was a shrine, worthy of pilgrimage.[38]

With no time to write during the intensity of the battle, Parker delayed corresponding to his sister until December 2, one week after the Union victory. "We have had a big fight here, which commenced on the 23rd ult. and lasted 5 days." He then recounted the engagement in infinite detail.[39] Parker concluded his extraordinary letter by describing the Confederates' wounding of a fellow staff officer from Batavia, the western New York town only fifteen miles from Parker's Tonawanda Reservation. The officer was struck by a shot from an Enfield rifle between the shoulders "which passed around his neck, coming out in front of the shoulder joint above the collar bone."[40]

In a subsequent letter to his brother Nicholson written from Nashville on January 25, Parker revealed further details about his illness, the Battle of Chattanooga, his impressions of the South, and his admiration for John Ross. His illness nearly resulted in his death: "my pulse apparently died out and my extremities began growing cold."

---

[37] Ely S. Parker to Caroline Parker Mountpleasant, Nov. 21, 1863.

[38] The sixteenth-century Creek town of Chiaha was "on an island near present day Chattanooga." Ronald N. Satz, *Tennessee's Indian Peoples: From White Contact to Removal, 1540–1840* (Knoxville, TN, 1979), 8. Despite writings to the contrary, the word "Chattanooga" is not of Cherokee language origin. Floyd Lounsbury to Laurence M. Hauptman, June 18, 1991, letter in author's possession. The late Dr. Lounsbury, Professor Emeritus of Anthropology at Yale University, was the foremost modern linguist of the Iroquoian languages, which includes Cherokee. For John Ross and Cherokee presence in late eighteenth- and early nineteenth-century Chattanooga, see Gary E. Moulton, *John Ross: Cherokee Chief* (Athens, GA, 1978), 5–6, 99.

[39] Ely S. Parker to Caroline Parker Mountpleasant, Dec. 2, 1863, APS.

[40] Ibid.

After recovering, he spent four days during the Battle of Chattanooga constantly on horseback, which ultimately led to a major "relapse of the shakes." Consequently, Parker was also "greatly reduced in flesh" as a result of this unidentified but debilitating illness; however, he insisted that he had finally recovered and apparently he was not beset by any further major health problems during the war.[41]

Parker then elaborated on his personal experiences in combat during the Battle of Chattanooga and graphically described the carnage. Because he was not in General Hooker's first advance, Parker had to ride approximately a kilometer while under the enemy's fire to get to Hooker's headquarters. While dodging bullets, shot, and shell for the first time, Parker nevertheless insisted that he "was not in the least afraid" but "greatly pleased at being in the midst of a battle." The Seneca officer then admitted that he had become hardened to the immense tragedy of the battlefield with its stacked bodies and putrid smells. According to Parker, he had ridden "over a battle field, among the dead, dying and wounded. I admit that it is a most shocking sight to look upon, but generally we have other and more important matters to think of, that does not permit us to yield to feelings of sympathy and pity."[42]

Linderman has suggested that Civil War soldiers' code of courage "ordained that the soldier react to the sights of the battlefield with *sang froid*, the ability to remain unmoved by the horrors of war."[43] On the surface, Ely S. Parker's behavior at the Battle of Chattanooga seems to fit Linderman's assessment. The Civil War did transform human beings into part of a vast army of war-machines intent on total war, destroying the enemy rather than simply winning battles; nevertheless, there is another logical explanation. Iroquois warriors in the beaver wars and wars out of Niagara were taught emotional restraint. Parker's numbness to the suffering around him was as much a product of his Seneca heritage as of his Civil War experience. Anthropologist Anthony F. C. Wallace has labeled this Iroquoian behavior the "ideal of autonomous responsibility." Besides being a good hunter, generous provider for his family and community, and "loyal and thoughtful friend and clansman," the warrior was also stern and

---

[41] Ely S. Parker to Nicholson Parker, Jan. 25, 1864, Ely S. Parker MSS., APS.
[42] Ibid.
[43] Linderman, *Embattled Courage*, 64.

ruthless in avenging injury. "And he was always stoical and indifferent to privation, pain, and even death."[44]

In sum, the Seneca officer, as did most non-commissioned Union Indian foot-soldiers, brought his own unique Native American heritage into Civil War combat. His letters reveal much about his Seneca ethnicity during the Civil War era. Memories of the nefarious Treaty of Buffalo Creek haunted Seneca life. During the war, Parker's frame of reference was always Seneca country and the Tonawanda Reservation. He measured the South and Southerners by those standards, which reflected his deep affection for the Indian path which he had taken in the first half of his life. Parker's writings, to a degree, reflect the common biases of most Northern men toward white and black rural Southerners; however, Parker's distinguished Seneca lineage, rooted in Iroquoian religion and politics, had as much to do with shaping his views as did other factors.

By the time of the Civil War, Iroquois reservations were hardly identical to other American communities. The Iroquois had been victimized from 1784 onward, losing over 95 percent of their homeland. Many had been removed to Indian and Wisconsin territories or had sought refuge in Canada. In 1861, the Iroquois were not citizens of the United States, and most did not choose to be. They were historically, legally, and racially distinct communities set apart from other Americans. Consequently, although at times their wartime experiences and attitudes about the "infernal rebels" paralleled those of many other Americans, they were not simply carbon copies of their non-Indian comrades in arms. Indians and non-Indians had distinctive reasons for joining military service and had varying experiences in the war. Most significantly, the Iroquois Indian experience was separate and distinct because they had to counter other challenges far from Southern battlefields. From 1838 to 1875, the Iroquois repeatedly had to fend off the grasping clutches of land speculators, railroad magnates, and state and federal officials intent on obtaining the Indians' shrinking land base. In effect, the Iroquois between 1861 and 1865 fought two wars, one in the South and the other on the home front.

---

[44] Wallace, *The Death and Rebirth of the Seneca*, 30–34.

5

Above the Law?
Arbitrary Arrests, Habeas
Corpus, and Freedom of the
Press in Lincoln's New York

Joseph W. Bellacosa

THANK YOU FOR THE *PRIVILEGES* of my inclusion in this outstanding symposium. I yearn for the associated *immunities*. This amateur and dabbler deems it quite daunting to dare step onto the "dialogue" stage—as Harold Holzer has so deftly characterized our engagement this Saturday afternoon—among life-long veteran experts and national specialists in the subjects at hand—like my friend and colleague Judge Frank Williams, who gets to speak after me and in defense of President Lincoln. Ah, but thanks be for the sweet solace of tenure, both judicial and academic—and the home court advantage.

As the designated proponent of the view that Mr. Lincoln acted "Above the Law" in regard to the suspension of the Great Writ of Habeas Corpus, I come before you today, nevertheless, not to tarnish his lionized reputation as Preserver of the Union and Emancipator of the Slaves. Rather, I venture forth in an effort to humanize and de-canonize Mr. Lincoln, not demonize him. We are here to explore the suspension of habeas corpus by executive fiats, not abstractly but within some larger historical perspective and with an eye to its precedential repercussions.

I choose, with a dash or play on words, to label my exertion The Principle of Expediency. Chief Justice Rehnquist's recent book captures the spirit of this topic, drawing on Mr. Lincoln's own piercing, well-invoked phrase: "[A]re all the laws, but one, to go unexecuted, and the government itself go to pieces, lest that one be violated?"[1]

For me, the artful title and theme I proffer—"The Principle of Expediency"—helps me to understand and perhaps even justify the broad-reaching and persistent suspension of the writ of habeas corpus in Lincoln's first years of the Civil War. Mr. Lincoln even used the word—"expediency"—twice in a great letter to Erastus Corning of Albany in 1863 (see Epilogue), to which I will return shortly in some detail.

I continue to believe and contend, nevertheless, that the actions Mr. Lincoln authorized were *ultra vires,* or at least excessive and over-broad, geographically and otherwise. They represent the use of raw, unilateral executive power, and questionable means to attain some debatable though desirable ends in a concededly horrific set of exigent circumstances that can only be fairly described as lessers among evil choices. I approach the question of our debate not from the technical, though important, location of the suspension power in the Articles that distribute and grant authority in our Constitution, but from a more overarching perspective.

First, a key historical, constitutional template and textual framework is useful to place before you. The three-fifths Compromise planted what I dub the Principle of Expediency—something of an oxymoron itself—into the central organic soil and document of this nation's governance from its very outset. So, it should come as no big surprise that expediency should emerge in later harvests—some very bitter—and in many profound permutations. Sadly, the principle, if I may continue to so dignify the word and idea of expediency, is not really or inherently contradictory. Regrettably, it is consistent in its human dimensions, or at least all too understandable in governmental affairs, underscored so substantially by compromise, consensus, and epistemology that guarantee that there are few, if any, moral absolutes in this realm of governance.

Second, a personality competitiveness is also at work, not unlike other momentous historical crises and clashes, to wit Chief Justice Roger Taney and President Abraham Lincoln, neither of whom liked

---

[1] Abraham Lincoln, Messages to Congress in Special Session (July 4, 1861), in Roy P. Basler, editor-in-chief *The Collected Works of Abraham Lincoln* 9 vols. (New Brunswick, NJ: Rutgers University Press, 1953–55) 4:421, 430.

or trusted the other. These two large figures seemed destined to be entwined and then entangled by earlier wary assessments of one another's actions, beliefs, and geographic and cultural predispositions and developments. The great cases and some of the other personality contests are all too familiar to you (e.g., *Luther v. Borden*[2]; *Dred Scott v. Sanford*[3]; *Ex parte Merryman*[4]; *Ex parte Milligan*[5]; see also, e.g., *Jefferson v. Marshall; Jackson v. Marshall; Theodore Roosevelt v. Holmes*.

As a third perspective, I tender a hard question. Was the real goal of this extraordinary deprivation of liberties and due process the lofty preservation of the Union—or was the activity a shield for suppressing powerful political opposition and dissenting expression and a sword for enforcing conscription? That is a mouthful; it is surely an essay question; and there is no facile answer. To be sure, mixed motives were at work.

I rather favor Mark Neely's book "The Fate of Liberty"[6] in its suggestion that there is persuasive proof that the writ suspension actions were to a significant extent politically motivated. The bold actions by Mr. Lincoln—but even more so those by his key cabinet officers Seward and Stanton, and most seriously and dangerously by the generals and subordinates all the way down the command line—demonstrated an indiscriminate breadth and delegation of execution of the Writ Suspension Orders, geographically, selection-wise, and otherwise.

These sweeping consequences make the continuing debate of our question not at all theoretical, even in this lively and important retrospective evaluation. Rather, the debate re-ignites powerfully personal, pervasive, and still vital and relevant issues for all of us to appreciate and assess the impact on the liberties of thousands of real people, individuals, past and present—and so that we might all be watchful guardians against violations and abuses in the future. We all have a role to play.

My fourth allusion is that this very day, June 12, 1999, on which we meet here in Albany is the anniversary—June 12, 1863—of Mr.

---

[2] 48 US 1 (1849).

[3] 60 US [19 How] 393 (1857).

[4] 9 Am Law Reg 524 (1861).

[5] 71 US [4 Wall] 2 (1866).

[6] Mark E. Neely, Jr., *The Fate of Liberty: Abraham Lincoln and Civil Liberties* (New York: Oxford University Press, 1991).

Lincoln's famous Defense Letter to Erastus Corning and others—Democrats—of Albany, New York. He answers their "censure" resolutions against him, the criticism of the day on the subject at hand, and then some. He cogently defends the Great Writ Suspension. His lengthy letter is extraordinary. It is at once a superb lawyer's brief and an exquisite Commander-in-Chief's resolute voice. As Jeff Shaara advised us last evening, hear Lincoln's own voice by reading the letter aloud to yourself some afternoon, evening, or morning. (See Epilogue.)

But for me, Mr. Lincoln's expressed skepticism, bordering on cynicism of the judiciary, is particularly unsettling in a phrase I extract from that letter. "Nothing is better known to history than that courts of justice are *utterly incompetent* to such cases"[7] (my emphasis). That is a dangerous proposition, especially taken out of its extended context. It is neither a lawyer's nor a statesman's remark. It is volatile rhetoric in the context of the Country's extreme trauma, to be sure; and it is very uncharacteristic of Mr. Lincoln and most of the rest of the letter, probably driven by his dislike, distrust, and defensiveness about Chief Judge Taney and his sympathizers.

This "utterly incompetent" quote evokes for me some illustrative references that heighten my concerns and may sharpen your consideration and evaluation in the precedential universe. I speak of precedent here in the executive action sense, not exclusively in the judicial stare decisis sense. The Principle of Expediency shows itself, here and there, at moments of greatest tension and testing in our history and cases as, for example, the following:

A. *Korematsu v. United States* and Justice Jackson's dissenting expression: "A military commander may overstep the bounds of constitutionality, and it is an incident. But if we review and approve, that passing incident becomes the doctrine of the Constitution. There it has a generative power of its own, and all that it creates will be in its own image."[8]

B. *Youngstown Sheet and Tube Co. v. Sawyer*—President Truman's seizure of the steel mills during the Korean War, and ironically his eventual clash and dispatch of General MacArthur, as in Taney versus Lincoln[9]

---

[7] Abraham Lincoln to Erastus Corning and Others (June 12, 1863), in Roy P. Basler, ed., *Abraham Lincoln: Speeches and Writings 1859–1865* (1989), 454, 457.

[8] 323 US 214, at 246 [1944][Jackson, J., dissenting].

[9] 343 US 579 (1952).

C. Muhammad Ali[10] and Julian Bond[11]—Vietnam and the draft and executive actions producing varied disqualifications and losses of personal liberties or entitlements

D. *Brown v. Board of Education*[12]—The Judicial Principle and Expediency exemplified through the decree but only "with all deliberate speed."

I tie this portion of my dialogue with a loose parallel from my own Third Branch experience, right here in Albany. It is of fairly recent and modern vintage in a state fiscal crisis of momentous and dangerous proportions and implications during the 1970s. It showed the Principle of Expediency at work in various ways in *Flushing National Bank v. Municipal Assistance Corp. for City of N.Y.*[13]

During New York City's fiscal crisis in the 1970s, the Legislature, in "Extraordinary Session," passed, at the governor's urging, the New York City Emergency Moratorium Act. It imposed a three-year moratorium on actions to enforce the city's outstanding short-term obligations, namely, tax anticipation notes, bond anticipation notes, revenue anticipation notes, and urban renewal notes. The faith and credit of neither the state nor the city was pledged to the new MAC obligations, but only certain revenues which the city might raise or receive from the state was to stand behind these substituted obligations. The Court of Appeals ultimately ruled that the Act violated the State Constitution by denying faith and credit through the payment postponement of short-term anticipation notes of the city.

The Moratorium had passed on November 13, 1975.

The Court of Appeals, through an opinion by Chief Judge Breitel, held the Moratorium unconstitutional on November 19, 1976. Thus, a year of expediency was bought while the case worked through the courts, as Felix Rohatyn remarked later. In the oral argument of the case, former Federal Judge Simon Rifkind, a lion of the Bar, rhetorically challenged the Court. He asserted they dare not declare the Act unconstitutional because to do so would cause blood to flow in the streets of his beloved city as all necessary services would grind to a halt. The rhetoric failed to deter the Court.

[10] *Ali v. Division of State Athletic Commn. of Dept. of State of State of N.Y.*, 316 F Supp 1246.
[11] *Bond v. Floyd*, 385 US 116 (1966).
[12] 347 US 483 (1954).
[13] 40 NY2d 731 (1976).

But, the Court added that it "would serve neither plaintiff nor the people of the City of New York precipitately to invoke instant judicial remedies which might give the city no choice except to proceed into bankruptcy."[14]

"Plaintiff and other noteholders of the city are entitled to some judicial relief free of throttling by the moratorium statute, but they are not entitled immediately to extraordinary or any particular judicial measures unnecessarily disruptive of the city's delicate financial and economic balance."[15] This ruling, intelligently, prudently, and expediently deployed, turned out to be the best fiscal medicine for recovery and long-term trust in the word of the government and the state constitution. It remains a great case, with great meaning and teaching power for me.

What meaning might we all derive from my perspective on the persisting debate concerning the suspension of the Great Writ? The Principle of Expediency is a constant because democracy is messy, and its servants and ministers are all too human. So far, though, no better form of government has been found—even when we endure a civil uprising of the magnitude of devastation of the Civil War!

Moreover, the principle of checks and balances is also a constant and eventually trumps, or at least tempers, expediency. Read Mr. Lincoln's own point in this regard on Jackson and New Orleans in the Corning Letter. The people of this nation can be justly proud and secure that *ALL* the laws, including and especially the Great Writ, will, in the long haul and in the end, prevail. That, too, is the proof and teaching of history. Mr. Lincoln preserved the Union, to be sure. But the Constitution, despite his expedient actions of the moment, ultimately preserves the people's rights, privileges, and immunities, albeit imperfectly and in halting or all good time. Mr. Lincoln deserves all the credit he earned for preserving the Union with his intelligent, powerful executive leadership. That legacy is not marred, but is realistically appraised by the verdict of history on his unilateral and widespread suspension of the Writ of Habeas Corpus. That verdict, in my view, is that he exceeded his constitutionally prescribed powers, albeit in the larger cause and for the expedient purpose.

---

[14] Ibid., 741.
[15] Ibid.

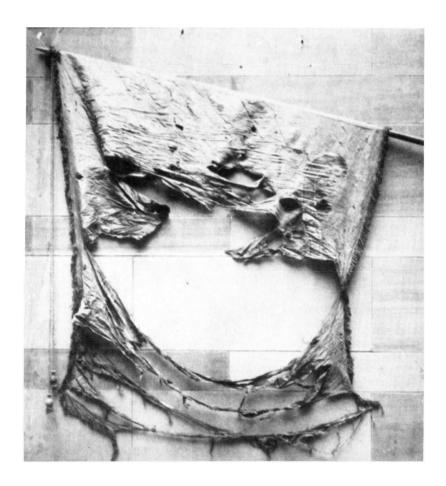

Colors of the 107th New York Volunteers (also known as the Campbell Guards), who fought at Antietam, Chancellorsville, and Gettysburg, as well as Sherman's Atlanta, Savannah, and Carolinas campaigns. This regimental standard shows the effects of an artillery shell that struck the flag while the regiment was engaged near the Dunker Church during the Battle of Antietam. (New York State Division of Military & Naval Affairs)

ATTENTION!
YOUNG MEN!

Recruits Wanted!
FOR THE
Wadsworth Guards!

Intelligent young men of sober and industrious habits, from 18 to 45 years of age, wishing to engage in the glorious cause of sustaining and defending our Constitution and the time honored old Stars and Stripes from the felonious hands of traitors and pirates, can have

THE BEST CHANCE YET OFFERED!
As it is organized under the immediate supervision of
GEN. JAS. S. WADSWORTH!
And attached to his Brigade. A Beautiful Camp has been established at Geneseo by especial permit from the Government, to be commanded by

COL. JOHN RORBACH!
RECRUITS TO RECEIVE
$100 BOUNTY.

Board and pay to commence as soon as enrolled. Recruiting Office in Hedges' Block, three doors below the Bank, Main Street, Dansville, N. Y.

W. T. LOZIER,
Recruiting Officer.

FOREST P. LOZIER,
Recruiting Sergeant.

GEORGE A. SANDERS, PRINTER, OFFICE OF THE DANSVILLE HERALD.

"Intelligent Young men of sober and industrious habits" ready to defend the Constitution "from the felonious hands of traitors"—and receive a $100 bounty in the bargain—are sought for the Wadsworth Guards in this early, extraordinary recruiting poster. The unit was encamped at upstate Geneseo, New York. (Manuscripts & Special Collections Unit, New York State Library)

The 1860 campaign poster—issued by H. H. Lloyd of New York City—that inspired eleven-year-old Grace Bedell of Westfield, New York, to write to candidate Abraham Lincoln suggesting he grow whiskers to hide his "thin" face. (Courtesy of The Lincoln Museum, Fort Wayne, Indiana [Ref. No. 394])

This 1862 lithograph by Sarony, Major & Knapp shows the departure of the 69th New York Regiment—the "fighting Irish"—from the old St. Patrick's Cathedral neighborhood in lower Manhattan in April 1861. New York's response to President Lincoln's early call for volunteers was both swift and strong. (Manuscripts & Special Collections Unit, New York State Library)

The United States Military Academy at West Point, New York, in an idyllic, pre-war engraving by J. Archer. The Academy trained a number of Union—as well as Confederate—generals. President Lincoln visited here in 1862 to meet with his aging former general-in-chief, Winfield Scott, who had retired there. (Manuscripts & Special Collections Unit, New York State Library)

Abraham Lincoln, the President Elect, Addressing the People from the Astor House Balcony, February 19, 1861, a woodcut illustration that graced the cover of the March 2, 1861 edition of *Harper's Weekly.* In truth, Lincoln's welcome in Democratic New York City, seen above, was far chillier than the hat-waving scene depicted here. (Library of Congress)

The *Funeral of Abraham Lincoln in New York,* as depicted in an 1865 lithograph by Currier & Ives, the New York printmaking firm. Lincoln's assassination and martyrdom erased partisan opposition to the wartime President overnight. More than 85,000 soldiers and civilians—including, by order of the Secretary of War, African Americans—marched in his funeral procession down Broadway. (Courtesy of The Lincoln Museum, Fort Wayne, Indiana [Ref. No. MA18])

The burning of the "Colored Orphan Asylum" on Fifth Avenue in Manhattan was one of the most brutal acts of violence of the draft riots. Its young occupants had to be shipped to a nearby island for safety. Here a group of men and women watch approvingly as the building goes up in flames. The woodcut appeared in the July 25, 1863 edition of the New York-based *Frank Leslie's Illustrated Newspaper.* (Manuscripts & Special Collections Unit, New York State Library)

THE MEETING OF THE FRIENDS,
CITY HALL PARK.

A FRIENDLY VOICE.—GOVERNOR, WE WANT YOU TO STAY HERE
HORATIO SEYMOUR.—I AM GOING TO STAY HERE, "MY FRIENDS."
SECOND RIOTER.—FAITH, AND THE GOVERNOR WILL STAY BY US.
HORATIO SEYMOUR.—I AM YOUR "FRIEND," AND THE "FRIEND" OF YOUR FAMILIES.
THIRD RIOTER.—ARRAH, JIMMY, AND WHO SAID HE CARED ABOUT THE "DIRTY NAGURS"?
FOURTH RIOTER.—HOW ABOUT THE DRAFT, SA'\MERE?
GOVERNOR.—I HAVE ORDERED THE PRESIDENT TO STOP THE DRAFT!
CHORUS.—BE JABERS, HE'S A "BROTH OF A BOY."

New York Governor Seymour's attempt to de-fuse the 1863 draft riots by addressing a mob as "my friends" came back to haunt the state's leading Democrat. Here a highly critical cartoon of the period shows him orating benignly while rioters commit horrendous atrocities against African Americans and a mob attacks the pro-Republican *New York Tribune* (background). (Manuscripts & Special Collections Unit, New York State Library)

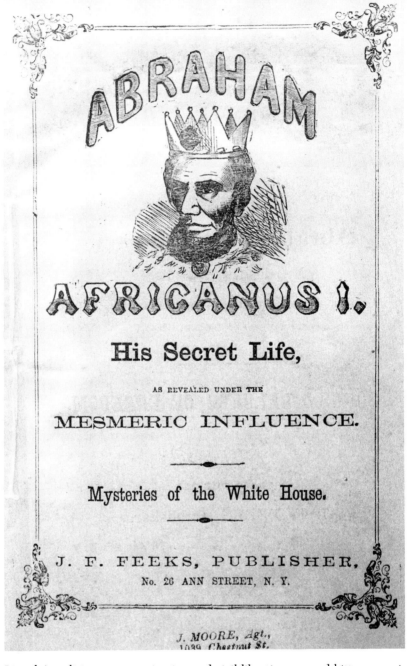

ABRAHAM
AFRICANUS I.
His Secret Life,

AS REVEALED UNDER THE

MESMERIC INFLUENCE.

Mysteries of the White House.

J. F. FEEKS, PUBLISHER,
No. 26 ANN STREET, N. Y.

J. MOORE, Agt.,
1039 Chestnut St.

Lincoln's policies on emancipation and civil liberties aroused bitter opposition in New York, where this pamphlet was published in time for the 1864 presidential election, during which Lincoln sought a second term. The cover illustration brands him as a self-crowned despot whose title, "Africanus," is clearly meant to hint ominously that his policies favored black, at the expense of white, Americans. (The Frank and Virginia Williams Collection)

INCOME TAX FOR 1862.

The Income Tax is imposed upon a certain proportion of the income of these two classes, viz:

1st. Every person residing in the United States; and every citizen residing abroad who is in the employment of the Government of the United States.

2d. Every citizen of the United States residing abroad, and not in the employment of the Government of the United States.

Every person in the *first* class will be taxed at the rate of *three* per cent. when his or her annual gains, profits, or income exceed $600, and do not exceed $10,000.

Every person in the *first* class will be taxed at the rate of *five* per cent. when the annual gains, profits, or income exceed $10,000, after the following deductions are made from the gross amounts returned, (as per table, page 2,) viz :

1st. The $600 allowed by law.

2d. Other national, State, and local taxes assessed for 1862, and paid.

3d. Rent actually paid for the dwelling-house or estate occupied as the residence of the person assessed.

4th. Necessary repairs to property yielding the income; or insurance thereon; or pay for hired laborers, and their subsistence, employed in conducting his business; or interest on incumbrances upon the property; or all, as the case may be.

Every person in the *second* class will be taxed at the rate of *five* per cent., whatever may be his or her annual gains, profits, or income from property, securities, and stocks owned in the United States, without other deductions than numbers 2 and 4 above stated.

Whenever the taxable income of a resident in the United States, ascertained as above, exceeds $10,000, and upon a portion of said amount three per cent. has been withheld by the officers of companies, corporations, and associations, from interest or dividends therein due him, such income will be subject to a tax of *two* per cent. additional upon so much thereof as may have been previously subjected to a duty of three per cent. by the officers of the companies, corporations, or associations aforesaid.

But in no case, whether a person is subject to a tax of three or five per cent., is a higher rate of tax than 1½ per cent. to be collected from that portion of income derived from interest upon notes, bonds, or other securities of the United States.

Where a husband and wife live together, and their taxable income is in excess of $600, they will be entitled to but one deduction of $600, that being the average fixed by law as an estimated commutation for the expense of maintaining a family. Where they live apart, by divorce or under contract of separation, they will be taxed separately, and be each entitled to a deduction of $600.

On the following pages will be found detailed statements to assist in making out returns.

An early publication of the rules governing the nation's first income tax—imposed during, and to help finance, the Civil War. This document entered New York State's vast Civil War collections generations ago. (Manuscripts & Special Collections Unit, New York State Library)

Lieutenant Cornelius C. Cusick was a Tuscarora Sachem and a heroic member of Company D of the 132nd New York Volunteers. (National Archives).

Colonel Ely S. Parker, a Seneca Sachem, served on General Grant's staff and witnessed Lee's surrender at Appomattox. (American Philosophic Society)

BATTLE OF CHATTANOOGA*

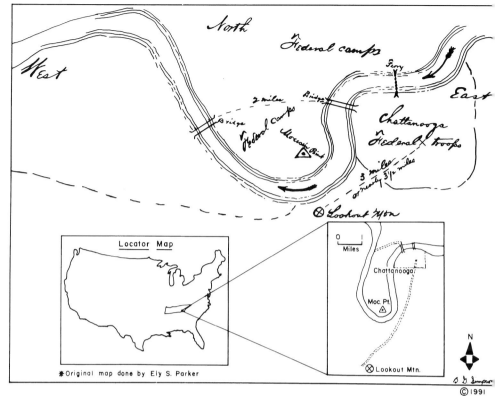

Locator Map

Miles

Chattanooga

Moc. Pt.

N

Lookout Mtn.

*Original map done by Ely S. Parker

©1991

Colonel Parker's hand-drawn map of the Battle of Chattanooga, November 1863. (American Philosophic Society)

The prison camp at Elmira, New York—a stockade no less disease-ridden and deadly for its prisoners than the more notorious Andersonville in Georgia—looks grim but oddly placid in this photograph. It was probably taken either just after the end of the war, or before its transformation from a recruiting barracks for Union recruits into a detention camp for Confederate prisoners. (New York State Division of Military & Naval Affairs)

Frederick Douglass, the most famous African-American leader of the Civil War era, had founded and for years edited the abolitionist newspaper the *North Star,* in Rochester. He was instrumental in recruiting so-called "colored" regiments of Union troops after 1863. Douglass debated the slavery issue in New York as early as 1843, in Buffalo; he chaired the National Convention of Colored Men at Syracuse in 1864. This characteristic pose was taken after the Civil War. It is one of hundreds of original cartes-de-visite to be found in a 27-volume collection assembled by Frederick Hill Meserve. (Manuscripts & Special Collections Unit, New York State Library).

Horace Greeley, the flamboyant New Hampshire-born editor of the *New York Tribune,* had been a New Yorker for thirty years when war broke out in 1861. An early advocate of emancipation and occasional critic of the Lincoln administration—though pro-Republican—Greeley would end his career on a bitterly ironic note: running unsuccessfully for President in 1872 as a Democrat against the greatest hero of the Civil War, Ulysses S. Grant. Greeley died shortly after his huge defeat. (Manuscripts & Special Collections Unit, New York State Library)

Erastus Corning, Albany Democratic Congressman, was a strong critic of Lincoln Administration policy on civil liberties. He helped organize the 1863 Albany convention that labeled Lincoln a tyrant for army prosecution of anti-war leader Clement L. Vallandigham of Ohio. The resolutions from that convention elicited Lincoln's famous reply to Corning and "others." (Manuscripts & Special Collections Unit, New York State Library)

MIGHTY PARTICULAR.

LITTLE MAC—" Yes, Mr. Vallandigham, I certainly took the situation of coachman, but I didn't know I was expected to drive such a wretched concern as that!"

The 1864 Democratic candidate for President, former commanding general and New York resident George B. McClellan (left), received his share of campaign criticism. Here, a cartoon from *Harper's Weekly* depicts him as a liveried coachman about to offer a ride in his "wretched," peace-driven carriage to the controversial Vallandigham, whom many Northerners believed no better than a traitor. (Courtesy of The Lincoln Museum, Fort Wayne, Indiana [Ref. No. 3534])

The House managers of the Andrew Johnson impeachment trial appear resolute and formidable in this formally-posed photograph, designed as the nineteenth-century equivalent of a publicity picture, to advance their cause. Seated second from left in the front row, holding his cane, is Speaker of the House Thaddeus Stevens. Elderly and infirm, he died shortly after his impassioned effort to remove Johnson from office failed. (Manuscripts & Special Collections Unit, New York State Library)

Andrew Johnson, the seventeenth president of the United States, as he looked shortly after Lincoln's assassination, which elevated him unexpectedly to the nation's highest office. Johnson would be impeached by the House of Representatives, but escape conviction and removal from office by a single vote. (Manuscripts & Special Collections Unit, New York State Library)

6

Rebuttal: Abraham Lincoln, Civil Liberties, and the New York Connection— The Corning Letter

Frank J. Williams

WARTIME PROCEDURES implemented by Abraham Lincoln suggest much about politics and philosophy. When the government of a democratic nation imposes harsh methods to sustain itself, there rightly will be sincere protest and criticism, and there will be slurs upon democracy itself. This criticism will endure if the nation survives, but suppose it does not survive. Suppose it fails because of internal division, dissension, or treason. In such cases, there will be greater criticism, stressing the weakness and inadequacy alleged to be characteristic of a democratic nation in an emergency.

In facing this situation, Lincoln was in a no-win position. He would be condemned, regardless of his actions. If he did not uphold all the provisions of the Constitution, he would be assailed not only by those who genuinely valued civil liberty, but also by enemies and opponents whose motive was criticism itself. Far harsher would have been his denunciation if the whole experiment of the democratic American Union failed, as seemed possible given the circumstances. If such a disaster occurred, what benefit would have been gained by adhering to a fallen Constitution? It was a classic example of the conflict: Do the ends justify the means?

Such, in part, was Lincoln's dilemma. To merely state the case in this way does not, however, exhaust the subject. Suppression is a matter of degree. To use a judicious amount of it does not imply rampant brutality, severity, and despotism. Measures regarded as severe in Lincoln's time would have seemed soft and "decadent" to a Hitler or a Milosevic. Congress continued to sit, elections were held, the Supreme Court functioned, lower courts sat, and dissent was allowed. It becomes, therefore, a matter of importance to examine the Lincoln procedures, to perceive them for what they were, to study them against the backdrop of those threatening times, and to note the qualifications, concessions, compromises, and ameliorations that appeared in the human application of measures that appear harsh when considered in isolation.

To speak of the government as Lincoln's is in part true and in part a matter of rhetoric. Abraham Lincoln was the nation's attorney-in-chief as well as its commander-in-chief. Much that happened was shaped by the force of personality, discretion, and executive procedure of the President. The Congress and military leaders took actions of which Lincoln disapproved.

In managing the government, Lincoln acted. He took authority; he was proactive; he did not depend upon Congress; he did not take his cues from the courts; he made the presidency, to a large extent, the dominant branch, certainly to a greater degree than it had normally been. Don E. Fehrenbacher, a noted Lincoln scholar, says that "Although Lincoln, in a general sense, proved to be right, the history of the United States in the twentieth century suggests that he brushed aside too lightly the problem of the example that he might be setting for future presidents."[1]

DEMOCRATIC LEADER OR DICTATOR?

In the words of James G. Randall, another pre-eminent Lincoln scholar: "No president has carried the power of presidential edict and executive order (independently of Congress) so far as he did. . . . It would not be easy to state what Lincoln conceived to be the limit of his powers."[2]

It has been noted how, in the eighty days between the April call for troops and the meeting of Congress on July 4, 1861, Lincoln per-

---

[1] Don E. Fehrenbacher, *Lincoln in Text and Context: Collected Essays* (Stanford, CA: Stanford University Press, 1987), 139.

[2] J. G. Randall, *Lincoln the Liberal Statesman* (New York: Dodd, Mead, 1947), 123.

formed a whole series of important acts by sheer assumption of presidential power. He proclaimed not "civil war" in those words, but the existence of "combinations too powerful to be suppressed by the ordinary course of judicial proceedings."[3] He called forth the militia to "suppress said combinations,"[4] which he ordered "to disperse and retire peacefully"[5] to their homes. Congress is constitutionally empowered to declare war, but suppression of rebellion has been recognized as an executive function, for which the prerogative of setting aside civil procedures has been placed in the President's hands. In this initial phase Lincoln also proclaimed a blockade, suspended the *habeas corpus* rights, increased the size of the regular army, and authorized the expenditure of government money without congressional appropriation. He made far-reaching decisions and commitments while Congress was not in session, and all without public polls. Lincoln could count, and he knew he had the votes of the Congress if not of the people. He put necessity above popularity, and suffered for it in the 1862 elections. The verdict of history is that Lincoln's use of power did not constitute abuse. Every survey of historians ranks Lincoln as number one among the great presidents, although he would not have fared as well had the war been lost.[6]

By the time of his inauguration on March 4, 1861, seven Southern states had already seceded from the Union. But Lincoln played a waiting game and made no preparation for the use of force until the sending of provisions to Fort Sumter in Charleston Harbor, a month later, precipitated its bombardment by the rebels. The situation had become unstable.

Now began Lincoln's period of executive decision. Congress was not in session at the time (nor would it meet until the special session of July 4), and it was basic to the Whig-Republican theory of govern-

---

[3] Roy P. Basler, editor-in-chief, *The Collected Works of Abraham Lincoln*, 9 vols. (New Brunswick, NJ: Rutgers University Press, 1953–55), 4:332 (hereafter cited as *Collected Works of Lincoln*).

[4] Ibid.

[5] Ibid.

[6] For example, see Arthur M. Schlesinger, Jr., "The Ultimate Approval Ratings," *New York Times Magazine* (December 15, 1996), 46–51. Lincoln did well, too, in a survey regarding famous people in the second millennium. He ranks thirty-second, behind Gutenberg (1) and Hitler (20). See Agnes Gottlieb, et al., *1,000 Years, 1,000 People: Ranking the Men and Women Who Shaped the Millennium* (New York: Kodansha International, 1998).

ment that Congress was vested with the ultimate power—a theory with which Lincoln, as both Whig and Republican, had long agreed. As a former member of Congress, four-term state legislator, and, for twenty-four years, a lawyer, Lincoln respected traditional separation of powers. But now, as he put it, "events have controlled me."[7]

SUSPENSION OF THE PRIVILEGE OF THE WRIT
OF *HABEAS CORPUS*

The state of Maryland was seething with secessionist tendencies almost more violent at times than some states that did secede. Events in Maryland ultimately provoked Lincoln's suspension of the writ of *habeas corpus*. The writ of *habeas corpus* is a procedural method by which one who is imprisoned can file the writ in an appropriate court to have his imprisonment reviewed. If the imprisonment is found not to conform to law, the individual is entitled to immediate release. With suspension of the writ, this immediate judicial review of the imprisonment is unavailable. This suspension triggered the most heated and serious constitutional disputes during the Lincoln administration.

On April 19, the Sixth Massachusetts militia arrived in Washington after having literally fought its way through Baltimore. On April 20, railroad communications with the North were severed by Marylanders, almost isolating the capital from the rest of the Union. Lincoln was apoplectic. He had no information about the whereabouts of the other troops promised him by Northern governors, and he told volunteers on April 24, "I don't believe there is any North. The Seventh Regiment is a myth. Rhode Island is not known in our geography any longer. *You* are the only Northern realities."[8] On April 25, the Seventh New York militia finally reached Washington after struggling through Maryland. The right of *habeas corpus* was so important that the President considered the bombardment of Maryland cities as preferable to the suspension of the writ, having authorized General Winfield Scott, Commander of the Army, in case of "necessity," to

---

[7] *Collected Works of Lincoln,* 4:344.
[8] Tyler Dennett, ed., *Lincoln and the Civil War in the Diaries and Letters of John Hay* (New York: Dodd, Mead, 1939), 11.

bombard the cities, but only "in the extremist necessity"[9] was Scott to suspend the writ of *habeas corpus*.

THE CASE OF JOHN MERRYMAN

In Maryland, there lived at this time a dissatisfied American named John Merryman. Merryman's dissent from the course being charted by Lincoln was expressed in both word and deed. He spoke out vigorously against the Union and in favor of the South, and recruited a company of soldiers for the Confederate Army. Merryman became their lieutenant drillmaster. Thus, he not only exercised his constitutional right to disagree with what the government was doing, but he engaged in raising an armed group to attack and destroy the government. This young man's actions precipitated legal conflict between the President and Chief Justice of the United States, Roger Taney. On May 25, 1861, Merryman was arrested by the military and lodged in Fort McHenry, Baltimore, for various alleged acts of treason. Shortly after Merryman's arrest, his counsel sought a writ of *habeas corpus* from Chief Justice Taney, alleging that Merryman was being illegally held at Fort McHenry. Taney, already infamous for *Dred Scott*,[10] took jurisdiction as a circuit judge. On Sunday, May 26, 1861, Taney issued a writ to fort commander George Cadwalader, directing him to produce Merryman before the Court the next day at 11:00 a.m. Cadwalader respectfully refused on the ground that President Lincoln had authorized the suspension of the writ of *habeas corpus*. To Taney this was blasphemy. He immediately issued an attachment for Cadwalader for contempt. The marshal could not enter the fort to serve the attachment, so the old justice, recognizing the impossibility of enforcing his order, settled back and produced the now-famous opinion *Ex Parte Merryman*.[11]

Notwithstanding the fact that he was in his eighty-fifth year, the Chief Justice vigorously defended the power of Congress alone to suspend the right to the writ of *habeas corpus*. The Chief took this

---

[9] *Collected Works of Lincoln*, 4:344.

[10] *Dred Scott v. Sanford*, 19 Howard 393 (1857).

[11] *Ex Parte Merryman* is reprinted in *The War of the Rebellion: A Compilation of the Official Records of the Union and Confederate Armies*, ser. II, vol. 1 (Washington, DC: Government Printing Office, 1880–1902), 578.

position in part because permissible suspension was in Article I § 9 of the Constitution, the section describing congressional powers. He ignored the fact that it was placed there by the Committee on Drafting at the Constitutional Convention in 1787 as a matter of form, not substance.[12] Nowhere did he acknowledge that a rebellion was in progress or that the fate of the nation was, in fact, at stake. Taney missed the crucial point made in the draft of Lincoln's report to Congress on July 4: "[t]he whole of the laws which I was sworn to [execute] were being resisted . . . by nearly one-third of the states. Must I have allowed them to finally fail of execution? . . . Are all the laws but one to go unexecuted, and the government itself go to pieces, lest that one be violated?"[13] This was Lincoln at his lawyer and politician best.

By addressing Congress, Lincoln ignored Taney. Nothing more was done about Merryman at the time. Merryman was thereafter released from custody and disappeared into oblivion. Congress, two years later, resolved the ambiguity in the Constitution and permitted the President the right to suspend the writ while the rebellion continued.[14]

Not least is the sense that we get, in a case like *Merryman*, of what a clash between the executive and the judiciary is actually like. This provides a healthy reminder of how much we usually rely, in the last resort, on executive submission in upholding the rule of law, as it is the executive branch that, under the Constitution, is responsible for enforcing the laws.

Nevertheless, five years later (after the Union victory and with a Lincoln appointee, Salmon P. Chase, as Chief Justice) the Supreme Court reached essentially the same conclusion as Taney in a case called *Ex Parte Milligan*. "The Constitution of the United States is a law for rulers and people, equally in war and in peace. . . . The Government, within the Constitution, has all the powers granted to it, which are necessary to preserve its existence."[15] *Habeas corpus* could be suspended, but only by Congress; and even then, the majority said, civilians could not be held by the Army for trial before a military

---

[12] Constitution, Art. I., Sec. 9.
[13] *Collected Works of Lincoln*, 4:429.
[14] *Habeas Corpus Act of March 3, 1863*.
[15] *Ex Parte Milligan*, 4 Wall. 2 (1866), 120–21.

tribunal, not even if the charge was fomenting an armed uprising in a time of civil war.

Lincoln never denied that he had stretched his presidential power. "These measures," he declared, "whether strictly legal or not, were ventured upon, under what appeared to be a popular necessity; trusting then, as now, that Congress would readily ratify them."[16] Lincoln thus confronted Congress with a *fait accompli*. It was a case of a President deliberately exercising legislative power, and then seeking congressional ratification after the event. Some, especially Democrats, adamantly believed that in doing so he had exceeded his authority.

The Supreme Court Sustains the President in the *Prize Cases*

The judiciary was allowed to speak to the constitutional issues. These constitutional questions—the validity of initial war measures, the legal nature of the conflict, Lincoln's assumption of war power—came before the Supreme Court in one of the classic cases heard by that tribunal. The decision in the *Prize Cases*[17] arose in March 1863, though the specific executive acts had been performed in 1861. The particular question before the Court pertained to the seizure of vessels for violating the blockade whose legality had been challenged since it was set up by presidential proclamation in absence of a congressional declaration of war. The issue, however, had much broader implication, since the blockade was only one of the emergency measures Lincoln took by his own authority in the "eighty days."

It was argued in the *Prize Cases* that Congress alone had power to declare war, that the President had no right to institute a blockade until after such a declaration, that war did not lawfully exist when the seizures were made, and that judgments against the ships in lower Federal courts were invalid. Had the high court in 1863 decided according to such arguments, it would have been declaring invalid the basic governmental acts by which the war was waged in its early months, as well as the whole legal procedure by which the govern-

---

[16] *Collected Works of Lincoln*, 4:429.
[17] *Prize Cases*, 67 U.S. 635 (1863).

ment at Washington had met the 1861 emergency. The matter went even further and some supposed that a decision adverse to the President's excessive power would have overthrown, or cast into doubt, the legality of the whole war.

Pondering such an embarrassment to the Lincoln administration, the distinguished lawyer Richard Henry Dana, Jr., wrote to Charles Francis Adams: "Contemplate, the possibility of a Supreme Court deciding that this blockade is illegal! . . . It would end the war, and how it would leave us with neutral powers, it is fearful to contemplate!"[18]

Given these circumstances, it was a great relief to Lincoln and his administration when the Court sustained the acts of the President, including the blockade. A civil war, the Court held, does not legally originate because it is declared by Congress. It simply occurs. The "party in rebellion" breaks its allegiance, "organized armies, and commences hostilities." In such a case it is the duty of the President to resist force by force, to meet the war as he finds it "without waiting for Congress to baptize it with a name." As to the weighty question whether the struggle was an "insurrection" or a "war" in the full sense (as if between independent nations), the Court decided that it was both.[19]

Lincoln's acts were thus held valid, the blockade upheld, and the condemnation of the ships sustained. It was a narrow victory. The decision, handed down on March 10, 1863, was five to four, and Chief Justice Taney was among the dissenters. Again, Lincoln was not Don Quixote—he would count popular, congressional, and judicial votes. He had stacked the Court in his favor. His appointments were decisive in their votes.[20]

EMANCIPATION AS A MILITARY MEASURE

Another illustration of Lincoln's legal and political astuteness relates to emancipation. The problem was prodigious. Nothing in the Con-

---

[18] James G. Randall, *Constitutional Problems Under Lincoln*, rev. ed. (Urbana: University of Illinois Press, 1951), 52.

[19] Ibid., 71–72.

[20] Justice Robert C. Grier delivered the majority opinion. Three Lincoln appointees joined him: Noah H. Swayne, Samuel F. Miller, and David Davis. Loyal Justice James M. Wayne of Georgia agreed with the majority.

stitution authorized the Congress or the President to confiscate property without compensation. When the preliminary Emancipation
Proclamation, issued on September 22, 1862, declared slaves in the
states still in rebellion to be free on January 1, 1863, the legal basis
for this action seemed obscure. Lincoln cited two acts of Congress
for justification.[21] Although reference to the two acts occupied much
of the proclamation, they actually had little to do with the subject,
indicating that Lincoln had not really settled in his own mind the
extent of his power, and on what authority to issue the Proclamation.
But, by the time of the final Emancipation Proclamation on January
1, 1863, Lincoln had concluded his act to be a war measure taken by
the Commander-in-Chief to weaken the enemy.

> Now, therefore, I, Abraham Lincoln, President of the United States,
> by virtue of the power in me vested as Commander-in-Chief, of the
> Army and Navy of the United States, in time of actual armed rebellion
> against authority and government of the United States, and as a fit and
> necessary war measure for suppressing said rebellion, do order . . . and
> declare that all persons held as slaves within said designated States,
> and parts of States, are, and henceforward shall be free. . . .[22]

It may have had all "the moral grandeur of a bill of lading," as
Professor Richard Hofstader stated,[23] but the basic legal argument
for the validity of his action could be understood by everyone. And
the time was ripe. To a hypothetical critic he wrote:

> You dislike the emancipation proclamation; and, perhaps, would have
> it retracted. You say it is unconstitutional—I think differently. I think
> the constitution invests its commander-in-chief, with the law of war, in
> time of war. The most that can be said, if so much, is that slaves are
> property. Is there—has there ever been—any question that by the law
> of war, property, both of enemies and friends, may be taken when
> needed? And is it not needed whenever taking it, helps us, or hurts
> the enemy?[24]

---

[21] "An Act to make an additional Article of War," March 13, 1862, and "An Act to
Suppress Insurrection, to Punish Treason and Rebellion, to seize and confiscate
property of rebels, and for other purposes," July 17, 1862; *Collected Works of Lincoln*, 5: 434–435.

[22] *Collected Works of Lincoln*, 6:29–30.

[23] Richard Hofstader, *The American Political Tradition* (New York: Vintage Books,
1974), 169.

[24] *Collected Works of Lincoln*, 6:408.

This is the Lincoln that consistently took the shortest distance between two legal points. The proposition as a matter of law may be argued. But it is not the law being analyzed, but rather Lincoln's political *and* legal approach to it. Lincoln saw the problem with the same directness with which he dissected most problems: the Commander-in-Chief may, under military necessity, take property. Slaves were property. There was a military necessity. Therefore, Lincoln, as Commander-in-Chief, took the property. Not only could Lincoln count votes, he could reason clearly even during a crisis.

VALLANDIGHAM AND THE CORNING LETTER

Clement Laird Vallandigham, the preeminent Copperhead[25] of the Civil War, was perhaps President Lincoln's sharpest critic. An Ohioan, this man whom Lincoln called a "wily agitator"[26] found many substantial supporters for his views in New York State. Active in politics throughout most of his life, he was elected to Congress from Ohio in 1856, 1858, and 1860. Before he was defeated for the 38th Congress in 1862, he returned to Ohio to seek the Democratic nomination for governor. In Congress he made a bitter political speech on July 10, 1861, criticizing Lincoln's inaugural address and the President's message on the national loan bill. He charged the President with the "wicked and hazardous experiment" of calling the people to arms without counsel and authority of Congress; with violating the Constitution in declaring a blockade of Southern ports; with "contemptuously" setting at defiance the Constitution in suspending the writ of *habeas corpus*; and with "cooly" coming before the Congress and pleading that he was only "preserving and protecting" the Constitution and demanding and expecting the thanks of Congress and the country for his "usurpations of power."[27]

---

[25] Copperhead, a reproachful epithet, was used to denote Northerners who sided with the South in the Civil War and were therefore deemed traitors, particularly those so-named Peace Democrats who assailed the Lincoln administration. It was borrowed from the poisonous snake of the same name that lies in hiding and strikes without warning. However, "Copperheads" regarded themselves as lovers of liberty, and some of them wore as a lapel pin the head of the Goddess of Liberty cut out of the large copper penny minted by the federal treasury.

[26] *Collected Works of Lincoln*, 6:266.

[27] *Congressional Globe*, 37 Cong., 1 sess., 23, 100, 348. See also Frank L. Klement, *The Limits of Dissent: Clement L. Vallandigham and the Civil War* (New York: Fordham University Press, 1998).

In his last extended speech in Congress on January 14, 1863, Vallandigham reviewed his lifelong attitude on slavery and espoused the extreme Copperhead doctrine when he said:

> [N]either, sir, can you abolish slavery by argument. . . . The South is resolved to maintain it at every hazard and by every sacrifice; and if "this Union cannot endure 'part slave and part free,' then it is already and finally dissolved . . . . But I deny the doctrine. It is full of disunion and civil war. It is disunion itself. Whoever first taught it ought to be dealt with not only as hostile to the Union, but as an enemy of the human race. Sir, the fundamental idea of the Constitution is the perfect and eternal compatibility of a union of States 'part slave and part free.' . . . In my deliberate judgment, a confederacy made up of a slaveholding and non-slave-holding States is, in the nature of things, the strongest of all popular governments.[28]

Later that year, on March 25, 1863, Union General Ambrose E. Burnside took command of the Department of the Ohio with headquarters at Cincinnati. Burnside, who had succeeded McClellan in the command of the Army of the Potomac, had failed miserably against General Robert E. Lee at Fredericksburg. He was smarting from defeat and anxious to repair his military reputation. The seat of the Copperhead movement was in this area. Wholesale criticism of the war was rampant. It was particularly offensive to Burnside at this time. On March 21, the week after Vallandigham's return from Washington and four days before Burnside took command of the Department of the Ohio, Vallandigham made one of his typical speeches at Hamilton, Ohio. On April 13, General Burnside, without consultation with his superiors, issued his famous General Order No. 38, in which he announced that all persons found within the Union lines committing acts for the benefit of the enemies of the country would be tried as spies or traitors, and, if convicted, would suffer death.[29] The order enumerated the various classes of persons falling within its scope, and announced that the habit of declaring sympathy for the enemy would not be allowed in the Department and that persons committing such offenses would be at once arrested with a view to being tried or banished from the Union lines.

Learning that Vallandigham was to speak at a Democratic mass

---

[28] *Congressional Globe*, 37 Cong., 2 sess., Appendix, 52–60.
[29] Klement, *Limits of Dissent*, 149.

meeting at Mt. Vernon, Ohio, on May 1, Burnside dispatched two captains in civilian clothes from his staff to listen to Vallandigham's speech. One of the captains leaned against the speaker's platform and took notes. The other stood a few feet from the platform in the audience. As a result of their reports, Vallandigham was arrested in his home at Dayton, on Burnside's orders, early after midnight on May 5 and escorted to the military prison, Kemper Barracks, at Cincinnati. On May 6 and 7, he was tried by a military commission convened by General Burnside, found guilty of violation of General Order No. 38, and sentenced to imprisonment for the duration of the war.[30]

On the first day of his imprisonment, Vallandigham smuggled out a message "To the Democracy of Ohio," in which he protested that his arrest was illegal and arose for no other offense than an expression of his "political opinion." He urged his fellow Democrats to "stand firm" and assured them, "As for myself, I adhere to every principle, and will make good through imprisonment and life itself, every pledge and declaration which I have ever made, uttered or maintained from the beginning."[31] Vallandigham's counsel applied to the United States Circuit Court sitting at Cincinnati for a writ of *habeas corpus*, which was denied. This time, unlike *Merryman*, the Court agreed with the suspension. An application was made later for a writ of *certiorari* to bring the proceedings of the military commission for review before the Supreme Court of the United States. This application was denied, too, on the ground that the Supreme Court had no jurisdiction over a military tribunal.[32]

General Burnside approved the finding and the sentence of the military commission and made plans to send Vallandigham to Fort Warren, Boston Harbor, for imprisonment. Before these plans could be carried out, President Lincoln telegraphed an order that commuted the sentence to banishment from Union lines.[33]

In conformity with the President's order, Vallandigham was conducted by way of Louisville, Kentucky, and Murfreesboro, Tennessee, to the Confederate lines. He arrived at the headquarters of

---

[30] Ibid., 152–68.
[31] Ibid., 163–64.
[32] Ibid., 171. The Supreme Court would exercise such jurisdiction after the war in *Ex Parte Milligan*.
[33] Ibid., 177–78.

General Braxton Bragg on May 25. Upon reaching the Confederate outpost and before the Federal officers left him, Vallandigham stated: "I am a citizen of Ohio, and of the United States. I am here within your lines by force, and against my will. I therefore surrender myself to you as a prisoner of war."[34] Vallandigham soon found his way to Richmond where he was received indifferently by the Confederate authorities, and the fiction that he was a prisoner of war was maintained. Having resolved before leaving Cincinnati to endeavor to go to Canada, Vallandigham, without interference, took passage on June 17 on the blockade runner *Cornubia* of Wilmington, bound for Bermuda, arriving on June 20. After ten days in Bermuda he went by steamer to Halifax, arriving on July 5. He then found his way to Niagara Falls, Canada. He settled at Windsor, opposite Detroit, where he remained until returning to Ohio on June 15, 1864.

The arrest, military trial, conviction, and sentence of Vallandigham aroused excitement throughout the country. Criticism of Burnside for issuing General Order No. 38 and for using it against Vallandigham was widespread. President Lincoln was also severely criticized for not countermanding the sentence instead of commuting it. The general dissatisfaction with the case was not confined to the radical Copperheads. Many conservative Democrats, loyal supporters of the government in the prosecution of the war, were disturbed. Many Republican newspapers joined in questioning the action. Public meetings of protest were held in many cities. One of the most dignified and impressive protest meetings was held by the Democrats of Albany, New York, on Saturday evening, May 16, 1863, three days before Lincoln altered Burnside's sentence of imprisonment and ordered that Vallandigham be sent beyond Federal lines. Held in front of the capitol in the park, it was presided over by the Hon. Erastus Corning, a distinguished congressman from Albany. The meeting was endorsed by Democratic Governor Horatio Seymour who, unable to attend, sent a letter which said: "The action of the Administration will determine in the minds of more than one half of the people of the loyal States whether this war is waged to put down rebellion at the South, or to destroy free institutions at the North. We look for its decision with the most solemn solicitude."[35]

34 Ibid., 181–83.
35 Ibid., 180–81.

Fiery speeches criticized Burnside for his action against Vallandigham, and pent-up feeling was expressed against the alleged arbitrary action of the Administration in suppressing the liberty of speech and of the press, the right of trial by jury, the law of evidence and the right of *habeas corpus*, and, in general, the assertion of the supremacy of military over civil law. A series of resolutions was adopted by acclamation and it was ordered that a copy of these resolutions be transmitted "to his Excellency the President of the United States, with the assurance of this meeting of their hearty and earnest desire to support the Government in every Constitutional and lawful measure to suppress the existing Rebellion."[36] Bearing the date of May 19, 1863, the resolutions were addressed to the President along with a brief note signed by Erastus Corning as president of the assemblage and by the vice-presidents and secretaries. The resolutions were couched in dignified and respectful language, but were clear that those attending the meeting regarded the arrest and imprisonment of Vallandigham illegal and unconstitutional, and deplored the abridgement of personal rights by the Administration.[37]

On May 28, 1863, the President acknowledged receipt of the resolutions in a note addressed to "Hon. Erastus Corning" and promised to "give the resolutions consideration" and to try "to find time and make a respectful response."[38]

There is no record that Lincoln was consulted by General Burnside in advance of the issuance of General Order No. 38, nor upon the arrest, trial, and sentence of Vallandigham. Lincoln was, of course, thoroughly familiar with Vallandigham as leader of the Copperheads and with his criticisms of Lincoln's administration. If left to Lincoln, he doubtless would have counseled that Vallandigham be allowed to talk himself to death politically.

On June 12, 1863, the President sent his studied reply to the Albany Democrats addressed to "Hon. Erastus Corning & others" (see Epilogue). In a closely reasoned document of more than three thousand words, and in lawyer-like fashion, Lincoln justified the action of the Administration in the arrest, trial, imprisonment, and banishment of Vallandigham, and elaborated his view that certain proceedings are

---

[36] The Albany Resolves are in Edward McPherson, *The Political History of the United States of America During the Great Rebellion* (New York: 1864), 163.

[37] Ibid., 182. Klement, *Limits of Dissent*, 182.

[38] *Collected Works of Lincoln*, 6:235.

constitutional "when, in cases of rebellion or Invasion, the public Safety requires them, which would not be constitutional when, in absence of rebellion or invasion, the public Safety does not require them. . . ." The President defended the action not on free speech grounds but on the effects of such speech.[39]

The political instincts of the lawyer-President emerged in Lincoln's reply when he said:

> In giving the resolutions that earnest consideration which you request of me, I cannot overlook the fact that the meeting speak as "Democrats." Nor can I, with full respect for their known intelligence, and the fairly presumed deliberation with which they prepared their resolutions, be permitted to suppose that this occurred by accident, or in any other way than that they preferred to designated themselves "democrats" rather than "American citizens." In this time of national peril I would have preferred to meet you upon a level one step higher than any party platform. . . .[40]

Erastus Corning referred Lincoln's response to the committee that reported the resolutions. Under the date of July 3, Mr. Corning forwarded to the President the rejoinder of the committee, a document of more than 3,000 words. This rejoinder dwelt at length upon what it deemed "repeated and continued" invasions of constitutional liberty and private right by the Administration and asked anew what the justification was "for the monstrous proceeding in the case of a citizen of Ohio." The rejoinder, drawn mainly by an ex-justice of the State Court of Appeals, John V. L. Pruyn,[41] did not maintain the even dignity of the original resolutions, charged Lincoln with "pretensions to more than regal authority,"[42] and insisted that he had used "misty and cloudy forms of expression"[43] in setting forth his pretensions. The committee was especially sensitive of Lincoln's remark that the resolutions were presented by "Democrats" instead of by "American

---

[39] Ibid., 267.

[40] Ibid., 267.

[41] John V. L. Pruyn et al., *Reply to President Lincoln's Letter of 12th of June 1863, Papers from the Society for the Diffusion of Political Knowledge*, no. 10 (New York, 1863). The pamphlet is in Frank Freidel, *Union Pamphlets of the Civil War, 1861–1865* (Cambridge: Harvard University Press, 1967), 760 (page references are to that reprint).

[42] Ibid., 755.

[43] Ibid.

citizens"[44] and sought to turn the tables on the President. Lincoln was too busy with a thousand other issues to engage in prolonged debate. As was his wont, he had his say in his reply in the initial resolutions; he ignored this rebuttal and turned to other matters.

Almost simultaneously, Lincoln was engaged in a parallel encounter with Democrats in Ohio. The Ohio Democratic State Convention, held at Columbus on June 11, 1863, while Vallandigham was still within the Confederate lines, nominated him for governor by acclamation. George E. Pugh, Vallandigham's lawyer in the *habeas corpus* proceedings, was nominated for lieutenant governor. The convention passed a series of resolutions condemning the arrest, trial, imprisonment, and banishment of Vallandigham and appointed a committee of 19 members to communicate with the President and to request the return of Vallandigham to Ohio. The committee, all of them members of Congress, addressed their communication from Washington on June 26 "To His Excellency the President of the United States."[45] The committee called on the President at the White House and filed with him its protest, including the detailed resolutions adopted by the Ohio Democratic State Convention. The resolutions were similar in import to those adopted by the Albany Democrats and held that "the arrest, imprisonment, pretended trial and actual banishment of Clement L. Vallandigham" was a "palpable" violation of the Constitution.[46] The committee went on to elaborate its view that the Constitution is not different in time of insurrection or invasion from what it is in time of peace and public security.[47]

Employing the arguments used in his letter to the Albany Democrats and not departing from the principles there expressed, Lincoln very promptly replied to the Ohio committee. He added "a word" to his Albany response:

> You claim that men may, if they choose, embarrass those whose duty it is, to combat a giant rebellion, and then be dealt with in turn, only as if there was no rebellion. The constitution itself rejects this view. The military arrests and detentions, which have been made, including those of Mr. V. which are not different in principle from the others,

[44] Ibid., 763.
[45] James Laird Vallandigham, *A Life of Clement L. Vallandigham* (Baltimore: Turnbull Brothers, 1872), 305.
[46] Ibid., 304.
[47] Ibid., 305–311.

have been for *prevention*, and not for *punishment*—as injunctions to stay injury, as proceedings to keep the peace. . . .[48]

In concluding his reply, Lincoln introduced a new and lawyer-like proposal. He insisted that the attitude of the committee encouraged desertion and resistance to the draft and promised to release Vallandigham if a majority of the committee would sign and return to him a duplicate of his letter committing themselves to the following propositions:

1. That there is now a rebellion in the United States, the object and tendency of which is to destroy the national Union; and that in your opinion, an army and navy are constitutional means for suppressing the rebellion.
2. That no one of you will do anything which in his own judgment, will tend to hinder the increase, or favor the decrease, or lessen the efficiency of the army or navy, while engaged in the effort to suppress that rebellion; and,
3. That each of you will, in his sphere, do all he can to have the officers, soldiers and seamen of the army and navy, while engaged in the effort to suppress the rebellion, paid, fed, clad, and otherwise well provided and supported.[49]

The Ohio committee was prompt in their rejoinder to Lincoln, dating their immediate response in a letter from New York City on July 1, 1863. The committee spurned Lincoln's concluding proposals and asked for the revocation of the order of banishment, not as a favor, but as a right, without sacrifice of their dignity and self respect. Lincoln did not reply to the rejoinder of the Ohio committee.

Safe in his retreat in Canada, Vallandigham accepted the nomination for governor of Ohio by the Democratic State Convention in an impassioned address by letter "To the Democrats of Ohio." The name of Burnside was "infamous forever in the ears of all lovers of constitutional liberty" and the President was guilty of "outrages upon liberty and the Constitution." Vallandigham's "opinions and convictions as to war" and his faith "as to final results from sound policy and wise statesmanship" were not only "unchanged but confirmed and strengthened."

The Democrats of Ohio carried on a vigorous campaign for the

---

[48] *Collected Works of Lincoln*, 6:303.
[49] Ibid., 305.

governorship. The Republicans nominated a former Democrat, John Brough, for governor. The keynote of the campaign was expressed by the Republican State Convention in the declaration and proposal that "in the present exigencies of the Republic we lay aside personal preferences and prejudices, and henceforth, till the war is ended, will draw no party line but the great line between those who sustain the government and those who rejoice in the triumph of the enemy."

The tone and temper of the Democratic campaign was typically illustrated in an address by George E. Pugh, candidate for lieutenant governor, at St. Mary's, Ohio, on August 15, 1863. *The Crisis* (Columbus, Ohio) for September 16 published the address in full. Pugh paid his compliments to Lincoln in language which outdid Vallandigham:

> Beyond the limits and powers confided to him by the Constitution, he is a mere County court lawyer, and not entitled to any obedience or respect, so help me God [Cheers and cries of "Good".] And when he attempts to compel obedience beyond the limits of the Constitution by bayonets and by swords, I say that he is a base and despotic usurper, whom it is your duty to restrict by every possible means if necessary, by force of arms. [Cheers and cries "That's the talk".] If I must have a despot, if I must be subject to the will of any one man, for God's sake let him be a man who possesses some great civil or military virtues. Give me a man eminent in council, or eminent in the field, but for God's sake don't give me the miserable mountebank who at present exercises the office of President of the United States.[50]

This extreme language, inspired originally by Vallandigham, no doubt contributed to the result of the election. The total vote in Ohio was more than 476,000. Brough received a majority of 61,752 at home and 40,000 in the armed forces. The Republicans won 29 of the 34 seats in the State Senate and 73 of the 97 in the House.[51]

One more formal effort was made in Vallandigham's behalf. On February 29, 1864, Congressman George H. Pendleton from Ohio offered the following resolution in the House of Representatives and moved the previous question for adoption:

> *Resolved* . . . That the military arrest, without civil warrant, and trial by military commission, without jury, of Clement L. Vallandigham, a citizen of Ohio, not in the land or naval forces of the United States, or the militia in active service, by order of Major General Burnside, and

---

[50] Klement, *Limits of Dissent*, 248.
[51] Ibid., 252.

his subsequent banishment by order of the President, executed by military force, were acts of mere arbitrary power, in palpable violation of the Constitution and laws of the United States.

The proposed resolution was killed by a vote of 37 to 35.[52]

VALLANDIGHAM AND NEW YORK

Vallandigham had visited New York State not long before his arrest in Ohio, and again shortly after returning from Canada. On each occasion he addressed large, sympathetic crowds.

In March 1863, before he celebrated his arrest, he had spoken to the Democratic Union Association in New York City, receiving "loud and protracted cheers." He then proceeded to Albany to confer "with leading men of the party on the state of the country." A few weeks later he was arrested at his home in Dayton, Ohio, on General Burnside's orders.

Ending his exile in mid-June 1864, Vallandigham was soon back on the oratorical platform. The first meeting he addressed outside Ohio was at Syracuse on July 18—"the number in attendance estimated at seventy-five thousand," an improbable estimate as the Syracuse census of 1865 showed a population of 32,000.

In the presidential contest of 1864, Vallandigham campaigned in New York State and elsewhere in support of General McClellan. His last visit to the state is believed to have taken place in 1868 when he attended the Democratic National Convention in New York City.

THE DOCTRINE OF NECESSITY

The crux of Lincoln's policy was his support of the doctrine of necessity. In his view, the civil courts were powerless to deal with the insurrectionary activities of individuals, saying, "he who dissuades one man from volunteering, or induces one soldier to desert, weakens the Union cause as much as he who kills a Union soldier in battle. Yet this dissuasion, or inducement, may be so conducted as to be no defined crime of which any civil court would take cognizance."[53] He knew that as President he had to act.

---

[52] *Congressional Globe*, 38 Cong., I Sess., 859 (1864).
[53] *Collected Works of Lincoln*, 6:264.

In his most famous passage on the subject, contained in the Corning Letter, Lincoln stated eloquently:

> Must I shoot a simple-minded soldier boy who deserts, while I must not touch a hair of a wiley [*sic*] agitator who induces him to desert? This is none the less injurious when effected by getting a father, or brother, or friend, into a public meeting, and there working upon his feelings, till he is persuaded to write the soldier boy, that he is fighting in a bad cause, for a wicked administration of a contemptible government, too weak to arrest and punish him if he shall desert. I think that, in such a case, to silence the agitator, and save the boy, is not only constitutional, but, withal, a great mercy.[54]

CONCLUSION

What made Lincoln a successful Commander-in-Chief was his constitutional flexibility, which allowed him to bend the Constitution within the framework of his wise, honest, restrained temperament without breaking it. Lincoln the lawyer-President avoided narrow overemphasis, and understood the difference between distortion for personal aggrandizement and clarification for a higher purpose—that of preserving the greatest legal framework ever devised: the Constitution. Lincoln alternately preached to the American people and ordered arms to fulfill the true destiny of the Union as "the last best hope of earth."[55] He could not have done this had he not been first a lawyer, and then a president. Rather than limit himself to the role of Commander-in-Chief or attorney-in-chief, he used his background to deliver the greatest performance of his life in the courtroom of world opinion. In his "Epilogue" to his *Fate of Liberty*, Mark E. Neely, Jr., closes by saying "If a situation were to arise again in the United States when the writ of *habeas corpus* were suspended, government would probably be as ill-prepared to define the legal situation as it was in 1861. The clearest lesson is that there is no clear lesson in the Civil War—no neat precedents, no ground rules, no map. War and its effect on civil liberties remain a frightening unknown."[56]

President Lincoln knew and understood this.

---

[54] Ibid., 266.

[55] Ibid., 5:537.

[56] Mark E. Neely, Jr., *The Fate of Liberty: Abraham Lincoln and Civil Liberties* (New York: Oxford University Press, 1991), 235.

7

New York's Andersonville: The Elmira Military Prison

Lonnie R. Speer

EVEN BEFORE THE END of the Civil War, the P.O.W. camp at Andersonville, Georgia, had become symbolic of the terrible conditions experienced by thousands of Union soldiers held by the Confederacy. At the time, and for many years afterward, the general public was led to believe that no similar places existed for Union-held P.O.W.s in the North, despite the accounts of those who had experienced such places. Well into the 1880s, and even into the 1950s, Andersonville was believed to be in a class by itself. Today, however, we realize that there were prisoner-of-war camps in the North that were as bad as any in the South. Among the worst of these was the camp at Elmira, New York.

Though outwardly very different in appearance from Andersonville, and much smaller in prisoner population, the conditions—and even the death rate—at Elmira were remarkably similar to those at Andersonville. Established about five months after the notorious Georgia prison, Elmira, like Andersonville, received many P.O.W.s—often in poor health—from other overcrowded prisons.

Elmira was one of the three original military depots established in the state to muster and train recruits.[1] The Elmira depot consisted of four large camps known as Barracks No. 1, No. 2, No. 3, and No. 4. Barracks No. 1, known locally as Camp Rathbun, was located near the Northern Central Railroad shops. Barracks No. 2 was in Arnot field, south of Washington Avenue and east of Lake Street. Barracks No. 3 was situated on West Water Street above Hoffman, along the Chemung River, and Barracks No. 4 was located a mile and a half

---

[1] Established on July 30, 1861. The other two depots were in Albany and New York City.

southwest of town. Barracks No. 3, officially known to the federal government as "Post Barracks," was eventually chosen as the prison site.

"[It is on] a plot of ground quite level, not easily drained and considerably lower than the surrounding country," according to the original report. "In consequence . . . [it] becomes at wet seasons quite soft and muddy. . . . The water from the wells on the grounds and from the junction canal south of it is unfit for use and must be hauled."[2] Unlike the other three Elmira posts, which were situated on higher ground with better water supplies, about a third of this site would remain wet, soggy, and—due to a stagnant pond or lagoon—unhealthy.[3] As at Andersonville, a flash flood would wreak havoc on the site during one point of the prison's existence.

Post No. 3 consisted of twenty 88' × 18' barracks designed to house 100 men each. Each building contained two small rooms, one measuring 24' × 7' and the other 8' × 5'. Upon conversion to prison use, additional bunks three tiers high and running the length of each room were constructed, bringing the capacity of each building to 150, or 3,000 for the entire prison. Construction of fifteen additional barracks measuring 100' × 22', including a 20' × 22' kitchen in each, brought the total prison capacity to 5,250. However, Federal authorities continued to refer to the prison's official capacity as 8,000 to 10,000 in official reports.[4]

These barracks, one-story structures of rough wood, often referred to as "sheds" by the Commissary General of Prisoners,[5] were mere shells, uninsulated and without interior walls or ceilings. Such construction was of little consequence to the prisoners during the warm summer months but became a harsh environment with the onset of the frigid upstate winter. According to a number of prisoners' memoirs, snow and ice became common between December 6 and March 15, and it wasn't at all unusual to see Elmira's prisoners standing ankle-deep in the snow for roll calls during this period. "[F]or at least four months of every year," complained prisoner Anthony M. Keilley, "anything [here] short of a polar-bear would find locomotion impracticable." December 1864 and January 1865 were especially brutal;

---

[2] O.R., Ser. II, 4:70.
[3] Ibid., 67–75.
[4] O.R., Ser. II, 7:152, 157, 425.
[5] Ibid., 918

the temperature hovered below zero for quite some time and fell to eighteen below at least twice. "It was a pleasant summer prison for the southern soldiers," agreed prisoner John R. King, "but an excellent place for them to find their graves in the winter."[6]

Approximately 30 acres, consisting of the barracks and additional buildings, about eight acres of open ground for pitching tents, and the lagoon were all enclosed by a 12-foot-high stockade fence with a parapet around the outside for guards to patrol and to have an unobstructed view of the compound's interior. At even intervals, 24 sentry boxes were positioned along the parapet.

The first 399 prisoners arrived on July 6, 1864; 400 were transferred from the overcrowded Point Lookout prison in Maryland, but one escaped en route. Within a week, another 751 arrived. By the end of the month, nearly 4,500 P.O.W.s had been transferred to Elmira. Within that time, two had managed to escape and eleven had died. In addition, one of the trains bringing more P.O.W.s was wrecked at Shohola, Pennsylvania, killing 48 prisoners and 17 guards; 93 prisoners and 16 guards were seriously injured.

By the end of August, more than 9,600 P.O.W.s were confined at Elmira. The initial arrivals had filled the barracks, so tents were erected for the overflow. The supply of tents was quickly exhausted and many prisoners, poorly clad and many having no blankets, found themselves sleeping out in the open air with no shelter whatsoever. "Thinly clad as they came from a summer's campaign, many of them without blankets and without even a handful of straw between them and the [cold] earth," one prisoner observed, "it will surprise no one that the suffering, even at that early day, was considerable." Adding to the severe suffering and discomfort, winter came early to the area. "Last night and this morning was cold, the coldest weather I ever experienced in August," prisoner Wilbur W. Gramling noted in his diary on August 31, 1864, before he finally came down with pneumonia.[7]

---

[6] G. T. Taylor, "Prison Experience in Elmira, N.Y." *Confederate Veteran*, 20 (1912): 327; Matthew S. Walls, "Northern Hell on Earth," *America's Civil War* (March 1991), 25; Anthony M. Keiley, *In Vinculis: or The Prisoner of War, by a Virginia Confederate* (Petersburg, VA: Daily Index Office, 1866), 129; John Rufus King, *My Experience in the Confederate Army and in Northern Prisons* (Clarksburg, WV: Stonewall Jackson Chapter No. 1333 UDC, 1917), 36.

[7] Keiley, *In Vinculis*, 136; Wilbur W. Gramling, "W. W. Gramling Diary," *Southern Christian* (Macon, GA) *Advocate*, January 25, 1871.

By December, the suffering and fight for survival intensified. In addition to the various ailments from the cold, smallpox came to Elmira with the arrival of transferred prisoners from Governors Island. Within weeks it had swept through the prison to become an epidemic which led to a smallpox camp being established nearby. "[This] camp was several wall tents," advised prisoner Miles O. Sherrill, "with cots having two Confederates laying on each in reverse order—heads on opposite ends of the cot." Gramling noted forty cases of the disease in the prison by Christmas Eve of 1864 and learned that four of those had died. "Small pox is growing worse every day," he wrote on December 26. "Quite sickly in camp, from 15 to 25 die a day." According to the official records there were 397 cases of smallpox from December 1, 1864 to January 24, 1865. Union medical officials later admitted after the war that during this same period there were 1,738 on the sick list of the total prison population of 5,934 P.O.W.s at Elmira at that time, and due to the lack of adequate hospital accommodations many of those were left to suffer in their quarters. "They were dying by the hundreds here with small-pox and other diseases," insisted Sherrill. "The people at home never knew how we suffered in prison," lamented King. "If we attempted to tell it in our letters, the Censor saw that they were not mailed."[8]

Extending east and west across the south-central portion of the enclosure was a one-acre backwater lagoon of stagnant water that served as the prison's latrine and garbage dump. Originally named Foster's Pond, it began to radiate an offensive stench within five weeks of the arrival of the first prisoners. Before long it was nothing more than a large cesspool.

"[O]ne large sink used by the prisoners stands directly over the pond which receives [their] fecal matter hourly," complained the post surgeon, "[and] seven thousand men will pass 2,600 gallons of urine daily, which is highly loaded with nitrogenous material."[9] This lagoon varied from fifteen to thirty feet wide and from three to six feet deep. According to the post surgeon, the water remained a cloudy green

---

[8] Taylor, "Prison Experience," 327; Miles O. Sherrill, *A Soldier's Story: Prison Life and Other Incidents in the War of 1861–'65* (Raleigh: n.p., 1911), 11–12; Gramling, "Diary"; Joseph K. Barnes, ed., *The Medical and Surgical History of the War of the Rebellion* (Washington, DC: GPO, 1876), Vol. 3, Part 5, 56; King, *My Experience*, 41.
[9] O.R., Ser. II, 7:604.

most of the time and, similar to Andersonville, the general area of the prison grounds surrounding the site remained soggy during wet seasons.[10]

Between August 13 and October 17 of 1864, Sanger filed nine separate reports to complain about the lagoon, insisting that if the pond was drained and the decaying matter removed, a major source of disease at the prison could be eliminated. His superiors, however, ignored his warnings.[11]

One benefit provided by the deplorable conditions of Foster's Pond was that it became a haven for rats, thus providing the prisoners with an abundant alternative food source to help supplement their diet. According to many prisoner memoirs, the rats tasted no different than squirrels. Elmira was just one of several Union prisons where the catching and eating of rats became quite common. "We invented all kinds of traps and deadfalls to catch rats," admitted one prisoner. "Many found an acceptable substitute in rats," admitted another.[12]

Clearly, the daily rations provided by the Elmira authorities were inadequate. As one prisoner dryly observed, "[It] seemed only enough to feed disease."[13]

At the beginning of the war, both sides fed their P.O.W.s the prescribed Army ration. But on July 7, 1862, Union authorities decided that it wasn't necessary for P.O.W.s to receive the same amount of food as soldiers in the field and cut the prisoners' rations in half. After much publicity and propaganda associated with the alleged mistreatment and starvation of P.O.W.s held in the South, Union authorities reduced rations by half again on June 1, 1864, in retaliation—in effect, providing only one-fourth of the original amount. These reductions caused the men to fall into a vicious cycle of starving, eating, and starving. They were unable to ration food from one issue to the next, often consuming whatever they got immediately.

---

[10] Ibid., 1092–93; Barnes, ed., *The Medical and Surgical History*, Vol. 3, Part 5, 56.

[11] O.R., Ser. II, 7:682; Andrew MacIsaac, "From Bangor to Elmira and Back Again: The Civil War Career of Dr. Eugene Francis Sanger," *Maine History*, 37 (Summer–Fall, 1997): 43.

[12] The others were Ft. Delaware, Point Lookout, Johnson's Island, and Camp Chase.; F. S. Wade, "Getting Out of Prison," *Confederate Veteran*, 34 (1926), 379; Keiley, *In Vinculis*, 146.

[13] Sherrill, *A Soldier's Story*, 10–11.

Further complicating the situation, Union authorities eliminated vegetables from the prisoners' diet, believing such food to be a luxury. By the time Dr. Sanger arrived at the prison, only a few weeks after it was first established, he faced an immediate, almost epidemic, outbreak of scurvy—from the lack of ascorbic acid provided by vegetables in the diet—among the prisoners. In a report on August 26, 1864, Sanger reported that of the 9,300 prisoners he examined, he found 793 cases of scurvy.[14]

It would seem that the Confederacy lacked the necessary food and other supplies for adequate care of their prisoners, owing to the blockade and the destruction of crops, processing facilities, and transport facilities. The Union, on the other hand, simply *refused* to provide adequate rations to its prisoners of war.

And, as at Andersonville, equally devastating to the prisoners was a flood that roared through the facility. At Elmira it occurred on the night of March 16, 1865. "There had been much snow during the winter," explained prisoner John R. King. "The snow melted rapidly and soon the little Chemung was raging. The water came into our prison higher and higher, and in a short time the small pox hospital across the creek had to be abandoned."[15]

The river continued to rage until its waters had invaded the entire camp and submerged nearly all of its buildings. "The lower bunks were submerged and the second row was threatened," declared King. "A great part of the prison wall was gone and we could see about half of the cookhouse extending above the water. . . . We were confined in the higher bunks for a day or two with nothing to eat or drink but the dirty river water. After the water receded men came into our [barracks] in row boats, passing near where we were 'roosting' [and] gave us something to eat." According to Gramling, the flood waters reached a depth of five feet, washing away some the fence, several buildings, and left a number of mess houses and cook houses in up to four feet of mud.[16]

DEATHS

In the majority of military prisons, both North and South, the first deaths and burials within the facilities did not occur until after the

---

[14] J. Michael Horigan, "Elmira Prison Camp—A Second Opinion," *Chemung Historical Journal* (March 1986), 3452.
[15] King, *My Experience*, 44–45.
[16] Ibid.; Gramling, "Diary."

prison had been in operation for at least several weeks—in some cases, several months. Elmira and Andersonville, however, were exceptions. At Andersonville, the first death occurred within 48 hours of the arrival of the first prisoners into the compound. (Ironically, it was a trooper of the 2nd New York Cavalry, Adam Swarner of Company H.) At Elmira, a death occurred en route to the prison, and within 72 hours of the first prisoners entering the camp, the first death occurred inside. By the end of August, only seven weeks after the prison was established, 115 deaths had occurred. In September, another 385 perished.[17]

The majority of these deaths occurred from diarrhea and dysentery. Exposure was, no doubt, a contributing factor. Scurvy, in epidemic proportion, also broke out during the month; by September 11, there were 1,870 reported cases. By November, pneumonia was rampant and by December smallpox began to appear throughout the compound. Before long, Elmira led all Northern prisons in its death rate; 750 men died during the following three months, and nearly 1,500 more in the following four—an average of more than ten per day.[18]

It has been reported that most of the medicine distributed by doctors at this prison was not given out, but was *sold* to the sick. Quinine, for example, was sold for about eight cents an ounce. Nor was the free medical assistance, when provided, always helpful. In one incident, a Dr. Van Ney was told by the post's chief surgeon to give "four or five drops of Fowler's Solution of Arsenic" to three P.O.W.s to help relieve their suffering. In his haste Van Ney wrote what appeared to be "45 drops" and handed the prescription to an orderly, who proceeded to follow the instructions as they appeared. The overdoses acted quickly and within a short time killed the three P.O.W.s.[19]

Union authorities gave Colonel Seth Eastman, the prison commandant, authority to lease a half-acre plot in Elmira's Woodlawn Cemetery to bury the dead. Eastman obtained the services of John W. Jones, a sexton of the First Baptist Church who lived nearby, to take charge of the Confederate burials. Paid $40 per month to dig the graves, Jones went on to do a meticulous job of keeping accurate death records throughout the existence of the prison. The first

---

[17] O.R., Ser. II, 8:997–98.
[18] James I. Robertson, Jr., *Soldiers Blue and Gray* (Columbia, SC: University of South Carolina Press, 1988), 204; O.R., Ser. II, 8:998–1002.
[19] Walls, "Northern Hell on Earth," 28.

P.O.W. burial at Elmira was that of Abner Prevett of Company I, 4th North Carolina Regiment, who died on the train en route to the prison on July 5, 1864. Prevett was buried at Elmira the following day as the first arrivals were led into the new prison facility. The first P.O.W. death inside the compound was that of William J. Stockdale, Company G, 52nd Virginia Regiment, on July 9, 1864.[20]

According to Jones's records, the largest number of burials in any one month was 491, in February 1865, and the most in any one day was 48, requiring eight trips of the dead-wagon. At the rate the Elmira P.O.W.s were dying, Jones barely averaged more than 16 cents per burial for all his hard work.[21]

Although the total number of prisoners held and the total number of deaths among them was much larger at Andersonville than at Elmira, the actual ratio of deaths to prison population was quite comparable. It is generally accepted that about 52,345 prisoners of war passed through the gates of Andersonville, of whom 12,919—24.7 percent—died. At Elmira, of the 12,123 P.O.W.s, 2,963 perished: 24.4 percent.[22]

One need not be a Confederate sympathizer to ask: Would it not have been easier for the North to house, care for, and feed 12,000 men than for the blockaded South to house, care for, and feed 52,000?

---

[20] Clay W. Holmes, *The Elmira Prison Camp* (New York: G. P. Putnam's Sons, 1912), 131.

[21] Ibid., pp. 379, 439, 450; O.R., Ser. II, 8:1001.

[22] The number of P.O.W.s held at Andersonville during that prison's existence is as various as the number of sources consulted. Totals range from 32,000 in early sources to 41,000 in later ones. The even higher total cited here was fully documented by the Wisconsin Andersonville Monument Commission in 1911. In U.S. Government sources it is simply stated that "more than 45,000" were held there.

8

New York and the Impeachment of Andrew Johnson

Hans L. Trefousse

IN THE WAKE of the Senate's acquittal of President William J. Clinton on February 12, 1999, it is essential to look back at the only other presidential impeachment in American history, that of Andrew Johnson in 1868. What was the legacy of that impeachment and trial? To what extent was the Empire State affected? And how can these experiences be applied today?

The impeachment of Andrew Johnson resulted from the struggle between the President and Congress about the process of Reconstruction. Johnson, who had always been a Democrat but had run for the Vice Presidency on the Unionist ticket, was determined to restore the seceded states as quickly as possible with as few conditions as feasible and without much regard for the rights of the freed people. For this policy, he had the support of the Democrats, who were anxious to increase their strength through the reappearance of Southerners in Congress. Congress and the Republicans, on the other hand, were unwilling to admit these states unless they offered a modicum of civil and political rights to the African Americans, partially for a real concern for the freed people and partially for political reasons. The blacks, after all, were the principal reliable source of support for the Republican Party in the South. And since in New York the city tended to be Democratic and most of the upstate counties Republican, the former usually sympathized with the President and the latter with Congress. This controversy between the two branches of government became more and more heated as time went on. The impeachment was the ultimate outcome.

Johnson's impeachment was no sudden affair. For over a year, the leading radical Republicans had attempted to oust him. None of these were from New York; Thaddeus Stevens hailed from Pennsylvania, Benjamin F. Butler and Charles Sumner from Massachusetts, and Zachariah Chandler from Michigan, but more conservative New York Republicans like Senators Roscoe Conkling and Edwin D. Morgan tended to go along with many of the radicals' demands. In January 1867, the Republican majority charged the House Committee of the Judiciary with investigating the question of impeaching the executive, and it held lengthy hearings without finding any palpable crime or misdemeanor on which to indict the President. The committee continued its investigations in the succeeding fortieth Congress, and after several additional weeks of inquiry, it adjourned without rendering a report, defeating a resolution of impeachment by a vote of five to four. An additional meeting of the committee in July reaffirmed this result. In November, however, Congressman John C. Churchill of New York, an Oswego attorney who later became a judge of state's supreme court, changed his vote.[1] As he explained later, in June and July he had believed Johnson was carrying out the legislation of Congress, but events since that time—presumably, the dismissal of radical generals—had caused him to change his mind, and the majority of the Committee reported a series of articles charging usurpation of power by restoring property to rebels, by abusing the pardoning, appointing, and veto powers, by interfering with elections, and by failing to carry out laws of Congress.[2] These charges were so weak that they were voted down by the full House of Representatives, much to the satisfaction of such influential New York papers as *The New York Times*, the *World*, and the *Herald*. "End of the Impeachment Folly," headlined the *Times*, mirroring the democratic *World*'s "End of the Impeachment Fiasco" and the *New York Herald*'s "The Impeachment Farce Ended." Even the *Tribune*, radical as it was, maintained that it was satisfied. "We have never felt that good would come from forcing upon the country an issue which could only postpone reconstruction, embarrass the finances, and perhaps impose upon us the responsibility of meeting a revolution," it wrote.[3] Thaddeus Stevens,

---

[1] Hans L. Trefousse, *Impeachment of a President: Andrew Johnson, the Blacks, and Reconstruction* (New York: Fordham Univ. Press, 1999), 54ff., 74–75, 105–107.

[2] *New York Tribune*, December 7, 1867; David Miller DeWitt, *The Impeachment and Trial of Andrew Johnson* (Madison: State Historical Society of Wisconsin, 1967), 298–300.

[3] *The New York Times*, December 9, 1867; *New York World*, December 9, 1867; *New York Herald*, December 8, 1867; *New York Tribune*, December 9, 1867.

the radical leader of the House, in the Committee on Reconstruction, which he chaired, made another attempt early in February 1868 after Johnson had quarrelled with U. S. Grant about the latter's handing over the War Department to him, but that effort also failed.[4] Only when Johnson on February 21 openly challenged the Tenure of Office Act by dismissing Secretary of War Edwin M. Stanton while Congress was in session did the effort to impeach the President finally succeed. Two days later, after lengthy debate, the House finally passed the resolution of impeachment by a strict party vote. It then appointed a committee to draw up the charges, nine of which, specifying the dismissal of Stanton and the appointment of Adjutant General Lorenzo Thomas as Secretary ad interim as well as one other concerning the putative violation of the so-called Command of the Army Act, were adopted by the House on March 2. Two additional charges—one accusing the President of delivering speeches derogatory of Congress, the other summing up the other ten and adding the accusation of failing to carry out the Reconstruction Acts—followed shortly afterward.[5]

These proceedings caused great excitement in the nation as a whole as well as in New York. The Union Republican Presidential Club of the City of New York called a meeting to rally the representatives of the people against the "traitor, usurper, and violator of the law" in its headquarters at Broadway and 23rd Street, where its president, Charles Spencer, delivered a fiery address and the organization adopted resolutions supporting the actions of the House. Meanwhile, some radical Democrats announced themselves ready to support the President with arms and called on followers to come to 208 Broadway to sign the declaration. Because of the incendiary nature of the call, its sponsor, Captain E. T. Tucker, was arrested, only to be released on his own recognizance. He then changed the declaration to read, "We, the undersigned, desirous of supporting the President of the United States in the lawful exercise of his constitutional authority, do subscribe our names."[6]

In spite of the fact that the President was being impeached principally for the alleged violation of the Tenure of Office Act, a measure

[4] *Chicago Tribune*, February 13, 14, 1868.

[5] Michael Les Benedict, *The Impeachment and Trial of Andrew Johnson* (New York: Norton, 1973), 100–18.

[6] *New York Herald*, February 26, 1868; *The New York Times*, February 26, 1868.

passed in 1867 to keep him from using his patronage powers by requiring the consent of the Senate for the dismissal of officers appointed by and with its consent, the public at large was fully cognizant of the fact that the real reason for the impeachment was the President's defiance of congressional Reconstruction. As he continued to insist on and act in accordance with his own conservative position, some radical congressmen became convinced that Reconstruction could not be carried out successfully as long as he remained in the White House.[7]

The explanation for Johnson's stubborn refusal to compromise with Congress lay in his past. A poor white, born in Raleigh, North Carolina, he was apprenticed to a tailor when he was ten. At fifteen he escaped from his difficult master and walked to Tennessee, eventually ssettling in Greenville, where he established a tailor shop. Completely unschooled, and illiterate until he was taught to read by his wife, Johnson entered politics as a Democrat and worked his way up from alderman to mayor to the lower and then the upper chamber of the legislature and to Congress. When in 1853 the Whigs tried to gerrymander him out of office, he ran for governor, won, and was reelected in 1855. In 1857 he became a United States Senator. Coming from a section that had few slaves and was Unionist, he remained loyal at the outbreak of the Civil War, a stand that made him popular in the North. Lincoln appointed him military governor of Tennessee, a position that enabled him to establish a stern Unionist rule, and in 1864 he was nominated for Vice President on the Union ticket.[8] A War Democrat, he was convinced that the seceded states were still members of the Union; as he had maintained in the famous Johnson–Crittenden resolutions of 1861, the war was being fought, not for the purpose of interfering with the rights or established institutions of the states but to maintain the supremacy of the Constitution and to preserve the Union, and that as soon as these objects were accomplished, the war ought to cease.[9] And he never changed his mind. Moreover, he was a racist who believed that "the black race of Africa were inferior to the white man in point of intellect—better calculated

---

[7] For example, Thaddeus Stevens. See Beverly Wilson Palmer, ed., *The Selected Papers of Thaddeus Stevens*, 2 vols. (Pittsburgh: Univ. of Pittsburgh Press, 1996), 2:235.

[8] Hans L. Trefousse, *Andrew Johnson: A Biography* (New York: Norton, 1989).

[9] Cong. Globe, 37th Cong., 1st Sess., 257–58.

in physical structure to undergo drudgery and hardship—standing, as they do many degrees lower in the scale of gradation that expressed the relative relation between God and all that he has created than the white man." Holding these opinions, which he never changed, he naturally clashed with any number of Congressmen with more liberal opinions.[10]

When he succeeded to the presidency following Lincoln's assassination, after a brief period of breathing fire against the Confederate leaders, he published his plan of Reconstruction, which demanded nothing more of the former rebels (with the exception of some fourteen exempted classes) than an oath of allegiance. He also suggested the ratification of the Thirteenth Amendment abolishing slavery, the repudiation of the Confederate debt, and the nullification of the secession ordinances, without insisting even on every one of these conditions. And the franchise was restricted to whites.[11]

But this was exactly what New York Democrats also desired. The suffrage issue in the Empire State became one of the most controversial problems in the constitutional convention of 1867, where the radicals hoped to change the uneven suffrage provisions of the state, which required a three years' residence of potential black voters as well the possession of $250 worth of property—restrictions that did not apply to whites. And to some extent, some dissatisfied Republicans, led by Thurlow Weed, were equally conservative.[12]

Johnson's reconstruction—or, rather, restoration—plan resulted in the return of Southern conservatives to power, the enactment of black codes virtually remanding freed persons to a condition not far removed from slavery, and the election of leading Confederates to Congress. That body, unwilling to permit the results of the Civil War to be overturned, refused to admit the Southern representatives and senators-elect and passed the Fourteenth Amendment, granting citizenship to African Americans and seeking to extend to them the

---

[10] Cong. Globe, 28th Cong., lst Sess., App. 95–98; *Cincinnati Enquirer*, September 30, 1865.

[11] Paul H. Bergeron, ed. (Leroy P. Graf and Ralph W. Haskins, eds. of early volumes), *The Papers of Andrew Johnson* (Knoxville: Univ. of Tennessee Press, 1967–), 8:128–31, 136–38; Trefousse, *Johnson*, 217ff., 229.

[12] De Alva Stanwood Alexander, *A Political History of New York*, 4 vols. (Port Washington, NY: Ira Friedman, 1969), 3:190; James C. Mohr, ed., *Radical Republicans in the North: State Politics During Reconstruction* (Baltimore: The Johns Hopkins University Press, 1976), 68–69.

equal protection of the laws. These rival schemes of Reconstruction were submitted to the voters in the strongly contested mid-term elections of 1866, in which the congressional Republicans prevailed, increasing their already more than two-thirds majority in both Houses.[13] In New York, the Republicans gained a great majority in both Houses of the legislature, re-elected Governor Reuben Fenton, and elected nineteen of thirty congressmen. But the Democrats rolled up a tremendous majority in New York City, where Johnson enjoyed considerable support.[14]

Undaunted by the electoral setback, Johnson refused to abandon his opposition to the proposed amendment, and Congress countered by seeking to restrict his powers as chief dispenser of patronage and commander-in-chief of the army and navy. Not only did it pass the Tenure of Office Act to curtail the former but also a measure requiring him to give orders to the army only through its commanding general, to be stationed in Washington. In addition, it called the 40th Congress into session on March 4, 1867, immediately after the expiration of the 39th Congress, in order to keep a close watch over the President's actions. And, overriding Johnson's vetoes, it passed the Reconstruction Acts, remanding the seceded states to military rule and requiring them to institute black suffrage and to ratify the amendment before they could be readmitted. To comply with this legislation, the President was called upon to appoint five military commanders for the South.

But the President now made a countermove. Secretary of War Edwin M. Stanton had long opposed his policies, and as soon as Congress had adjourned, Johnson dismissed him and appointed General Grant in his stead as secretary ad interim. In addition, he discharged various radical commanders in the South, whom he himself had appointed. When the Senate reconvened, in accordance with the Tenure of Office Act it rejected Johnson's dismissal of Stanton and appointment of Grant. Johnson, determined not to tolerate his opponent in the cabinet again, now openly defied the Tenure of Office

[13] Eric Foner, *Reconstruction: America's Unfinished Revolution 1863–1877* (New York: Harper & Row, 1988), 176–280.

[14] James C. Mohr, Civil and Institutional Reform in New York State, 1864–1868, Ph.D. thesis, Stanford University, 1969, 238–39; James C. Mohr, *The Radical Republicans and Reform in New York During Reconstruction* (Ithaca: Cornell University Press, 1973), 205.

Act. Once more dismissing Stanton, he appointed Lorenzo Thomas, the adjutant general of the army, as secretary of war ad interim. The impeachment and subsequent trial was the result.[15]

For New York Democrats, the impeachment came at a very convenient time. In the elections of 1867, they had recaptured the state assembly; the state conservative Republicans had bolted the party, and though the Democrats no longer endorsed the President, they were not unhappy about the division the impeachment was bound to create among their opponents.[16]

When the Senate received notice of the dismissal, New York's Senator Roscoe Conkling was in the midst of delivering a speech. He was suddenly interrupted. The Senate went into executive session and passed a resolution condemning the President's action. New York's Senator Morgan, however, refused to vote on this matter. In the meantime, in the House of Representatives, John Covode of Pennsylvania introduced a resolution of impeachment, which was referred to the Reconstruction Committee. The next day, Thaddeus Stevens reported this resolution to the full House and on February 24 a resolution for impeachment was adopted by a vote of 126–27.[17]

In New York, these events caused considerable excitement. They became the main topic of conversation, not least on Wall Street. The business community was divided; some thought nothing would happen, others worried about the impact on American securities abroad. The *Tribune* wrote that business believed it would benefit because stability would be restored to the government with Johnson's replacement, but its opinion was colored by its Republican outlook. The press tended to follow its political inclinations, *The New York Times* mildly approving of the course of Congress, the *Herald* thinking that the radicals, not Johnson, were guilty of conspiracy, the *Tribune* heartily favoring the course of Congress, and the *World* roundly condemning the process. "Impeachment is the extreme medicine of the Constitution to be used on great and weighty occasions for the cure

---

[15] Trefousse, *Johnson*, 272–313.

[16] Alexander, *Political History of New York*, 3:190; Jerome Mushkat, *The Reconstruction of the New York Democracy, 1861–1874* (Madison, NJ: Farleigh Dickinson University Press, 1981), 127–28.

[17] *New York Herald*, February 22, 1868; Edward McPherson, *The Political History of the United States of America During the Period of Reconstruction 1865–1870* (Washington, DC: Philp & Solomons, 1871), 262–63, 265–66.

of desperate distempers. . . . Who will pretend that the safety of the Government or the stability of our institutions is staked on the retention of Edwin Stanton as Secretary of War?" it wrote. In the rest of the state, the usual division according to political orientation also held. In Albany as in the metropolis it became the chief item of interest; according to *The New York Times*, nothing else was talked about, while Lt.Col. Eastman in Poughkeepsie offered the services of the 21st Regiment to preserve peace in Washington. The inveterate diarist George Templeton Strong was sure that Johnson would be convicted, a prediction widely shared by many Republicans.[18]

In the meantime, the trial in Washington began. The social and political event of the season, it became the main attraction in the city. Tickets for admission to Congress were eagerly sought after and carefully preserved after the event; the ladies in all their finery appeared in the chamber, and the public watched the proceedings with eager anticipation. After the eleven charges were presented to the Senate, that body transformed itself into a court presided over by the Chief Justice, Salmon P. Chase, and on March 13 the public eagerly awaited the appearance of the defendant. Yet his lawyers, one of the most prominent of whom was William Evarts of New York, the later Attorney General and Secretary of State of the United States, had not allowed him to testify in person, much to the disappointment of spectators.

In New York, the *Herald* had already called the whole thing a "farce," and although it predicted that the president could expect no mercy, it thought the proceedings would disgrace the Republican Party but not the Chief Executive.[19] The state Democratic Convention, meeting in Albany two days earlier and condemning the Republican majority, had already passed a Declaration of Principles. "To insure this fatal dominance in the pending canvass and to complete a full conspiracy to overthrow the government of our fathers," it stated, "they resolved to depose the President and install one of the chief conspirators in his place—an act which the conservative freemen of

[18] *New York Herald*, February 23, 26, March 3, 1868; *New York Tribune*, February 22, 24, 25, 27, 1868; *The New York Times*, February 25, 27, 1868; *New York World*, February 24, 1868; Allan Nevins and Milton Halsey Thomas, eds., *The Diary of George Templeton Strong*, abridged by Thomas J. Pressly (Seattle: University of Washington Press), 235; Trefousse, *Impeachment*, 155–57.

[19] Ibid., 151–53, 165; *New York Herald*, March 18, 1868.

New York declare to be without justification or plausible excuse, and denounce as an outrage without parallel in civilized government." Its president, Marshall B. Champlain, said that Congress, not the President, should be impeached.[20]

After the Senate, in reply to the demands of the defense for a delay of forty days, granted ten, the trial commenced on March 30. Benjamin F. Butler, one of the managers, delivered the opening speech; having decided to try the case like a "horse case," he declaimed that "by murder most foul" the President assumed his office and was "the elect of an assassin to that high office." This characterization was not too different from that earlier endorsed by the Union Republican Presidential Campaign Club of New York City.[21]

The trial itself offered few surprises; the facts were known; the question was merely whether Johnson's actions had been lawful or merited impeachment. As *The New York Times* stated, "the questions involved are . . . questions of Constitutional law. It is for an alleged violation of the Constitution that the President is arraigned by the House."[22] Yet as the trial went on, it was still widely believed that the President would be convicted, and his putative successor, Senator Benjamin F. Wade, the president pro tem. of the Senate, was already making plans for his cabinet. There were reports in New York that after his conviction, the Democrats would bring Johnson to the city and arrange for a great reception by the city council before letting him depart for the South.[23] But it was generally conceded that the outcome depended on the vote of a few "recusant" Republican Senators, as there were twelve conservatives and Democrats in the Upper House, and if seven Republicans voted "not guilty," the President would be acquitted. Among the Senators believed to be doubtful was Edwin Morgan of New York, whom the *New York Herald* granted

---

[20] *New York Herald*, March 12, 1868; *The New York Times*, March 12, 1868.

[21] *Trial of Andrew Johnson, President of the United States, Before the Senate of the United States, on Impeachment by the House of Representatives, for High Crimes and Misdemeanors*, 3 vols. (Washington, DC: Government Printing Office, 1868), 1: 34–83, 87–147 [hereafter cited as *Impeachment Trial*]; Benjamin F. Butler, *Butler's Book* (Boston: A. M. Thayer, 1892), 929.

[22] *The New York Times*, March 25, 1868.

[23] Adam Badeau, *Grant in Peace* (Hartford, Conn.: S. S. Scranton, 1887), 136–37; cf. John B. Alley to Butler, May 2, 1868, Benjamin F. Butler Papers, LC; James A. Rawley, *Edwin D. Morgan 1811–1883, Merchant in Politics* (New York: Columbia Univ. Press, 1955); *The New York Times*, May 10, 1868.

"high character," calling him a man of "integrity and purity of purpose." The paper surmised that he had to know that in November the state had voted against the radicals by a 50,000 majority, and that he had to see that impeachment was a great outrage. How would he vote? Little doubt was expressed about the other New York Senator, Roscoe Conkling, who, though not deemed a radical, was certain to vote with his party.[24]

Shortly before the vote, the overwhelmingly Democratic New York Assembly, about to adjourn, passed a series of resolutions derogatory of Congress, concluding "that the evidence elicited on the trial of President Johnson before the Court of Impeachment has established the innocence of that high functionary, and that his conviction would be regarded by the people as the false judgment of a partisan court, and as a crime against the form and being of a republican government." And as late as during the first week of May, the *Rochester Democrat* still regretted that there was no way of getting rid of an obnoxious President and expressed its conviction that Johnson had violated a law.[25]

At last, on May 16, when the crucial day of the ballot arrived, the Senate voted on the eleventh article, which summed up the other ten. In the presence of the diplomatic corps, the high officials of the government, and all the leading members of society in Washington— and everybody who had been able to secure a ticket—the Chief Justice intoned the formula, "Mr. Senator so-and-so, how say you? Is the respondent, Andrew Johnson, President of the United States, guilty or not guilty of a high misdemeanor, as charged in this article?" The dropping of a pin could have been heard in the chamber as Senator after Senator answered, and when Senator Edmund G. Ross of Kansas voted "not guilty," it became evident that if Peter G. Van Winkle of West Virginia remained in the President's camp, Johnson would not be convicted. Ross plus the certain pro-Johnson votes starting with the letter R made it unnecessary for others to defect from the party, and Johnson was acquitted by one vote—despite the fact that both New York Senators voted for conviction.

---

[24] Fernand Baldensperger, ed., *Georges Clemenceau, American Reconstruction 1865–1870* (New York: Da Capo Press, 1969, 179–80; New York *Herald*, April 21, 1868; David M. Jordan, *Roscoe Conkling, Voice in the Senate* (Ithaca: Cornell University Press, 1971), 101–102.

[25] *The New York Times*, May 6, 7, 1868.

After adjourning for the Republican convention in Chicago, where the New York delegates, though ready to support the position of the managers, opposed any allusion to the recusants, the impeachers tried again ten days later, this time on articles II and III, but the outcome was the same, and the court adjourned sine die.[26]

The result was known in New York shortly before 2 o'clock. In the words of George Templeton Strong, "the streets were full of newsboys whose extras confirmed the report. People gathered at the various newspaper offices, and the Democrats congratulated each other that Wade was not yet in the White House, while the radicals turned away with glum faces but silent lips." In the Wall Street area, there was little excitement, and the brokers returned to their tasks. Strong thought that the outcome would not hurt the Republican Party because Johnson had not become a martyr, while the *New York Tribune* thought that the party was now relieved of responsibility for the President. The demand for impeachment had been heeded, but, concluded the paper, "Let Messrs. Chase, Fessenden & Company take care of their man Johnson, while we organize for and make certain the joyful advent of GRANT AND VICTORY." Yet it called the result a "Tainted Verdict."[27] The *World* naturally hailed the stoppage "of this infamous impeachment outrage in mid-career" and what it called the preservation "to the country of the integrity of its Executive office and authority." The *New York Herald* expressed its satisfaction that the "Great Farce" was over.[28] The managers started a fruitless investigation of possible bribery of Senators and summoned, among others, Thurlow Weed, the New York "Wizard of the Lobby," whose *New York Commercial Advertiser* had strongly defended the President.[29]

Why did the Republican Party, despite tremendous pressure to do so, fail to muster the necessary votes to convict? Andrew Johnson himself had made a number of deals, especially with Senator James Grimes of Iowa. He promised Grimes not to interfere with Reconstruction any further and to appoint General John M. Schofield as

---

[26] *Impeachment Trial*, 2: 484–98; Trefousse, *Impeachment*, 167–68. The Chief Justice had demanded complete silence.

[27] *Strong, Diary*, 371–72; *New York Tribune*, May 17, 27, 1868.

[28] *New York World*, May 17, 1868; *New York Herald*, May 27, 1868.

[29] Glyndon G. Van Deusen, *Thurlow Weed, Wizard of the Lobby* (Boston: Little, Brown, 1947), 328–29.

secretary of war, whereupon Grimes and his friend William Pitt Fessenden of Maine voted for acquittal. In addition, many were loath to elevate Benjamin F. Wade to the presidency because the Ohio Senator was too radical for them, advocating, as he did, equal rights for women and a new deal for labor. Not least of all, the weakness of the case—a case made even weaker by the lack of skill of the prosecution—convinced many that the charges were largely political, and that the violation of the Tenure of Office Act constituted neither a crime nor a violation of the Constitution but merely a pretext for Johnson's opponents.[30] Several of the so-called recusants, Republicans who defied their party to vote for Johnson, believed that the tripartite system of government, the balance of power between executive, legislative, and judiciary, was in danger in an impeachment widely viewed as political. As Senator Lyman Trumbull, one of the seven, wrote, "once set an example of impeaching a President for what, when the excitement of the hour shall have subsided, will be regarded as insufficient causes, and no future President will be safe who happens to differ with the majority of the House and two-thirds of the Senate on any measure deemed by them important."[31]

In addition, many were loath to elevate Benjamin F. Wade to the presidency because the Ohio senator was too radical for them, advocating, as he did, equal rights for women and a new deal for labor. As Johnson had only some nine months of his term left, they thought it was better to leave Johnson in than to have Wade in the White House. Last but not least, the weakness of the case—Johnson had committed no crime and had not violated the Constitution, so that the charges were largely political, the violation of the Tenure of Office Act being seen as but an excuse to oust Johnson because of his opposition to congressional Reconstruction—convinced others. The managers, as the prosecution was called, were not skillful enough to overcome these factors.[32]

And what was the result and the legacy of the failure of the impeachment trial? In the first place, from then until December 1998 it became axiomatic that no President could be impeached for basically

---

[30] Trefousse, *Johnson*, 323–24, 330–31.
[31] *Impeachment Trial*, 3: 328.
[32] *Impeachment Trial*, 3: 16ff., 29–30, 147–50, 193–204; 319–28; Edmund G. Ross, *History of the Impeachment of Andrew Johnson* (Santa Fe: New Mexico Printing Co., 1896), 169.

political reasons, no matter what the token charges might be. And when the second presidential impeachment in American history, again for alleged offenses largely seen to be excuses for political differences, also ended in acquittal, this rule was, if anything, strengthened. It also became established, and reinforced in 1999, that impeachment could be resorted to only in cases that clearly meet the constitutional prescription of "treason, bribery, and other high crimes and misdemeanors." Finally, in 1868 the acquittal probably undermined the Reconstruction process before it had even fully started. Johnson was anxious to keep the South a "white man's country," and in fact, for many generations, he did so. But he himself was so weakened after the trial that even diplomatic enterprises, such as the Johnson-Clarendon Convention with Great Britain regarding Civil War damages, could not be brought to fruition.[33]

It might be concluded from all these facts that the impeachment had little effect upon the Empire State. Such a conclusion, however, would fail to take into account some important facts. There is no doubt that the results in New York mirrored, to some extent, those in the country at large. Already in the ascendancy, the Democrats were given an additional boost by the trial and its outcome, and the badly fractured Republican Party fractured further. The radicals' hope of dominating the party was already in shambles in early February, when the Conklingites undercut Fenton, and because of Thurlow Weed's efforts, the Republican convention endorsed the candidacy of U. S. Grant. The Democrats, meanwhile, greatly encouraged by the impeachment and in the majority in the assembly, now blocked all further radical reforms, particularly the removal of discriminatory voter qualifications for blacks; this was accomplished by separating measures proposed by the state constitutional convention in such a way as to render the suffrage proposal more vulnerable to defeat. In the summer of 1868, the Republican convention rejected the radical Horace Greeley's candidacy for governor, and the Democrat John T. Hoffmann was elected in November. Thus in New York, as in the

---

[32] *Impeachment Trial*, 3: 16ff., 29–30, 147–50, 193–204; 319–28; Edmund G. Ross, *History of the Impeachment of Andrew Johnson* (Santa Fe: New Mexico Printing Co., 1896), 169.

[33] Papers Relating to Foreign Affairs (Washington, DC: Government Printing Office, 1869), I:377–83, 400–405.

nation at large, the failure of the impeachment weakened the radical cause.[34]

Finally, it is of course interesting to compare the impeachment of Andrew Johnson with that of William J. Clinton. In both cases, the ostensible charges hid the real differences between Congress and the President. In 1868, the controversy between the two over Reconstruction was infinitely more compelling than the violation of the Tenure of Office Act (which was declared unconstitutional in 1926); in 1998, the political antagonisms between the Republican right and the administration was considered by many much more important than Clinton's perjury. In both cases, party pressure was immense. But in New York, in 1868 as in 1998, some Wall Street observers did not seem to display any special worries. Yet there were real differences. In 1868, the impeachers, with the Republicans in control of more than two-thirds of the Senate, thought that they had a good chance of convicting. In 1998, this seemed totally unlikely as the Republicans lacked the necessary two-thirds majority in the Senate. And while Johnson had not committed any indictable offenses, Clinton apparently had indeed perjured himself, although his misdeeds would hardly seem to fit the definition of "high crimes and misdemeanors." Furthermore, while in 1868 the public, especially in the North, largely tended to support impeachment, in 1998–99 it was opposed to it.

---

[34] Mushkat, *Reconstruction of the New York Democracy*, 127–28; Mohr, *Radical Republicans*, 268; Mohr, *Civil and Institutional Reform in New York State*, 128–39.

Epilogue

Abraham Lincoln's Letter to Erastus Corning and Other New York Democrats June 12, 1863

ON MAY 16, 1863, a group of enraged New York Democrats held a mass indignation rally in Albany, led by the prominent local leader Erastus Corning. There they passed a widely publicized resolution reproaching the Lincoln administration for the military arrest of a prominent anti-war Democrat, Congressman Clement Laird Vallandigham of Ohio. New York's Democratic governor, Horatio Seymour, had aroused the rally with a strong letter warning darkly that if the arrest were sustained, "our liberties are overthrown." The mass meeting enthusiastically obliged with a formal declaration that "the people of this State, by an emphatic majority, declared their condemnation of the system of arbitrary arrests, and their determination to stand by the Constitution."[1]

Vallandigham's seizure, trial, and conviction for speaking out in opposition to the draft—followed by President Lincoln's decision to banish the "Copperhead" leader to the Confederacy as punishment—had unleashed a small storm of protest. Albany's anti-Lincoln Democrats, led by Corning, bitterly opposed the President's suspension of the writ of habeas corpus to engineer these and similar so-called arbitrary arrests. Lincoln countered that suspension of this Constitutional guarantee was in fact specifically allowed by the Constitution itself in times of rebellion or invasion, and was therefore necessary to save the Union from enemies within.

Lincoln replied to the Albany resolutions on June 12 with a long, logical, and lucid argument in which he made a compelling case that he must suspend certain civil liberties temporarily in order to pre-

---

[1] John G. Nicolay and John Hay, *Abraham Lincoln: A History*, 10 vols. (New York: The Century Co., 1914 ed.), 7:341–343.

serve them for all time. The so-called "Corning Letter" ranks as one of Lincoln's most accomplished legal-moral arguments, a vigorous state paper that adroitly defended his entire war policy and also pointed out that the Administration's reaction to protest had in fact been quite restrained. The letter first appeared in the *New York Tribune* on June 15—Lincoln made certain that it was published—and was widely reprinted in the weeks to come. "So terse and vigorous" was the language, declared the President's admiring private secretaries when they attempted to excerpt the letter for their Lincoln biography, "that it is difficult to abridge a paragraph without positive mutilation. . . ."[2]

A frustrated Corning responded to Lincoln's tract with a brilliant letter of his own in which he termed Lincoln's arguments "a monstrous heresy . . . tending to the establishment of despotism," and predicted that "the American people will never acquiesce in this doctrine."[3] But although this rejoinder, too, was published, Lincoln's response has deservedly earned the greater reputation. Writing to the President a few days later, an admirer named William A. Hall praised Lincoln's Corning Letter as more valuable "to the cause than a victory," adding: "You have not left them a simple peg to hang on."

Within days, the *Tribune* ordered 50,000 copies printed in pamphlet form. "Your friends in New York are taking steps to give every soldier in the field a copy of it," Hall revealed. "In a word it has done us all great good. God bless you for this. . . ."[4]

Lincoln's Corning Letter—indeed his entire policy on civil liberties—has remained a matter of scholarly and legal debate ever since. Historians like J. G. Randall, Frank L. Klement, and Mark E. Neely, Jr., among others, have confronted the subject in succeeding generations.[5] Although Neely has convincingly demonstrated in recent years

[2] Ibid., 7:343.

[3] See Roy P. Basler editor-in-chief, *The Collected Works of Abraham Lincoln*, 9 vols. (New Brunswick, NJ: Rutgers University Press, 1953–55), 6:261.

[4] William A. Hall to Abraham Lincoln, June 15, 1863, Abraham Lincoln Papers, Library of Congress. Reprinted in Harold Holzer, ed., *Dear Mr. Lincoln: Letters to the President* (New York: Addison-Wesley, 1993), 128.

[5] See, for example, James G. Randall, *Constitutional Problems Under Lincoln* (New York: D. Appleton & Co., 1926), esp. 184; Frank L. Klement, *The Limits of Dissent: Clement Vallandigham and the Civil War* (Lexington: University of Kentucky Press, 1970; reprinted New York: Fordham University Press, 1998), and Mark E. Neely, Jr., *The Fate of Liberty: Abraham Lincoln and Civil Liberties* (New York: Oxford University Press, 1991).

that Lincoln was no tyrant, the debate continues. One thing, however, remains indisputable: the Corning Letter was one of the most important state papers Lincoln ever wrote, offering crucial insight into his deftly balanced management of domestic and war policy.

Since it was originally written to New Yorkers, this often neglected masterpiece is reproduced here (complete with Lincoln's occasional misspellings) as an essential document without which no study of the Empire State and the Civil War could hope to be complete.

Lincoln's Letter to Erastus Corning and Others

Hon. Erastus Corning & others

Executive Mansion
Washington [June 12] 1863.

Gentlemen

Your letter of May 19th., inclosing the resolutions of a public meeting held at Albany, N.Y. on the 16th. of the same month, was received several days ago.

The resolutions, as I understand them, are resolvable into two propositions—first, the expression of a purpose to sustain the cause of the Union, to secure peace through victory, and to support the administration in every constitutional, and lawful measure to suppress the rebellion; and secondly, a declaration of censure upon the administration for supposed unconstitutional action such as the making of military arrests.

And, from the two propositions a third is deduced, which is, that the gentlemen composing the meeting are resolved on doing their part to maintain our common government and country, despite the folly or wickedness, as they may conceive, of any administration. This position is eminently patriotic, and as such, I thank the meeting, and congratulate the nation for it. My own purpose is the same; so that the meeting and myself have a common object, and can have no difference, except in the choice of means or measures, for effecting that object.

And here I ought to close this paper, and would close it, if there were no apprehension that more injurious consequences, than any merely personal to myself, might follow the censures systematically cast upon me for doing what, in my view of duty, I could not forbear. The resolutions promise to support me in every constitutional and lawful measure to suppress the rebellion; and I have not knowingly employed, nor shall knowingly employ, any other. But the meeting, by their resolutions, assert and argue, that certain military arrests and proceedings following them for which I am ultimately responsible, are unconstitutional. I think they are not. The resolutions quote from the constitution, the definition of treason; and also the limiting safe-guards and guarrantees therein provided for the citizen, on trials for treason, and on his being held to answer for capital or otherwise infamous crimes, and, in criminal prossecutions, his right to a speedy and public trial by an impartial jury. They proceed to resolve "That these safe-guards of the rights of the citizen against the pretentions of arbitrary power, were intended more *especially* for his protection in times of civil commotion." And, apparently, to demonstrate the proposition, the resolutions proceed "They were secured substan-tially to the English people, *after* years of protracted civil war, and were adopted into our constitution at the *close* of the revolution." Would not the demonstration have been better, if it could have been truly said that these safe-guards had been adopted, and applied *dur-ing* our revolution, instead of *after* the one, and at the *close* of the other. I too am devotedly for them *after* civil war, and *before* civil war, and at all times "except when, in cases of Rebellion or Invasion, the public Safety may require" their suspension. The resolutions pro-ceed to tell us that these safe-guards "have stood the test of seventy-six years of trial, under our republican system, under circumstances which show that while they constitute the foundation of all free gov-ernment, they are the elements of the enduring stability of the Re-public." No one denies that they have so stood the test up to the beginning of the present rebellion if we except a certain matter at New Orleans hereafter to be mentioned; nor does any one question that they will stand the same test much longer after the rebellion closes. But these provisions of the constitution have no application to the case we have in hand, because the arrests complained of were not made for treason—that is, not for *the* treason defined in the constitution, and upon the conviction of which, the punishment is death—; nor yet were they made to hold persons to answer for any capital, or otherwise infamous crimes; nor were the proceedings fol-lowing, in any constitutional or legal sense, "criminal prossecutions."

The arrests were made on totally different grounds, and the proceedings following, accorded with the grounds of the arrests. Let us consider the real case with which we are dealing, and apply to it the parts of the constitution plainly made for such cases.

Prior to my instalation here it had been inculcated that any State had a lawful right to secede from the national Union; and that it would be expedient to exercise the right, whenever the devotees of the doctrine should fail to elect a President to their own liking. I was elected contrary to their liking; and accordingly, so far as it was legally possible, they had taken seven states out of the Union, had seized many of the United States Forts, and had fired upon the United States' Flag, all before I was inaugerated; and, of course, before I had done any official act whatever. The rebellion, thus began soon ran into the present civil war; and, in certain respects, it began on very unequal terms between the parties. The insurgents had been preparing for it more than thirty years, while the government had taken no steps to resist them. The former had carefully considered all the means which could be turned to their account. It undoubtedly was a well pondered reliance with them that in their own unrestricted effort to destroy Union, constitution, and law, all together, the government would, in great degree, be restrained by the same constitution and law, from arresting their progress. Their sympathizers pervaded all departments of the government and nearly all communities of the people. From this material, under cover of "Liberty of speech" "Liberty of the press" and *"Habeas corpus"* they hoped to keep on foot amongst us a most efficient corps of spies, informers, supplyers, and aiders and abettors of their cause in a thousand ways. They knew that in times such as they were inaugerating, by the constitution itself, the "Habeas corpus" might be suspended; but they also knew they had friends who would make a question as to *who* was to suspend it; meanwhile their spies and others might remain at large to help on their cause. Or if, as has happened, the executive should suspend the writ, without ruinous waste of time, instances of arresting innocent persons might occur, as are always likely to occur in such cases; and then a clamor could be raised in regard to this, which might be, at least, of some service to the insurgent cause. It needed no very keen perception to discover this part of the enemies' programme, so soon as by open hostilities their machinery was fairly put in motion. Yet, thoroughly imbued with a reverence for the guarranteed rights of individuals, I was slow to adopt the strong measures, which by degrees I have been forced to regard as being within the exceptions of the constitution, and as indispensable to the public Safety. Nothing is better known to history than that courts of justice are utterly incompetent to such cases. Civil courts are organized chiefly for trials of individuals, or, at most, a few individuals acting in concert; and this in quiet times, and on charges of crimes well defined in the law. Even in times of peace, bands of horse-thieves and robbers frequently grow too numerous and powerful for the ordinary courts of justice. But what comparison, in numbers, have such bands ever borne to the insurgent sympathizers even in many of the loyal states? Again, a jury too frequently have at least one member, more ready to hang the panel than to hang the traitor. And yet again, he who dissuades one man from volunteering, or induces one soldier to desert, weakens the Union cause as much as he who kills a union soldier in battle. Yet this dissuasion, or inducement, may be so conducted as to be no defined crime of which any civil court would take cognizance.

Ours is a case of Rebellion—so called by the resolutions before me—in fact, a clear, flagrant, and gigantic case of Rebellion; and the provision of the constitution that "The previlege of the writ of Habeas Corpus shall not be suspended, unless when in cases of Rebellion or Invasion, the public Safety may require it" is *the* provision which specially applies to our present case. This provision plainly attests the understanding of those who made the constitution that ordinary courts of justice are inadequate to "cases of Rebellion"— attests their purpose that in such cases, men may be held in custody whom the courts acting on ordinary rules, would discharge. Habeas Corpus, does not discharge men who are proved to be guilty of defined crime; and its suspension is allowed by the constitution on purpose that, men may be arrested and held, who can not be proved to be guilty of defined crime, "when, in cases of Rebellion or Invasion the public Safety may require it." This is precisely our present case—a case of Rebellion, wherein the public Safety does require the suspension. Indeed, arrests by process of courts, and arrests in cases of rebellion, do not proceed altogether upon the same basis. The former is directed at the small per centage of ordinary and continuous perpetration of crime; while the latter is directed at sudden and extensive uprisings against the government, which, at most, will succeed or fail, in no great length of time. In the latter case, arrests are made, not so much for what has been done, as for what probably would be done. The latter is more for the preventive, and less for the vindictive, than the former. In such cases the purposes of men are much more easily understood, than in cases of ordinary crime. The man who stands by and says nothing, when the peril of his government is discussed, can not be misunderstood. If not hindered, he is sure to help the enemy. Much more, if he talks ambiguously—talks for his country with "buts" and "ifs" and "ands." Of how little value the constitutional provision I have quoted will be rendered, if arrests shall never be made until defined crimes shall have been committed, may be illustrated by a few notable examples. Gen. John C. Breckienridge, Gen. Robert E. Lee, Gen. Joseph E. Johnston, Gen. John B. Magruder, Gen. William B. Preston, Gen. Simon B. Buckner, and Comodore [Franklin] Buchanan, now occupying the very highest places in the rebel war service, were all within the power of the government since the rebellion began, and were nearly as well known to be traitors then as now. Unquestionably if we had seized and held them, the insurgent cause would be much weaker. But no one of them had then committed any crime defined in the law. Every one of them if arrested would have been discharged on Habeas Corpus, were the writ allowed to operate. In view of these and similar cases, I think the time not unlikely to come when I shall be blamed for having made too few arrests rather than too many.

By the third resolution the meeting indicate their opinion that military arrests may be constitutional in localities where rebellion actually exists; but that such arrests are unconstitutional in localities where rebellion, or insurrection, does not actually exist. They insist that such arrests shall not be made "outside of the lines of necessary military occupation, and the scenes of insurrection." In asmuch, however, as the constitution itself makes no such distinction, I am unable to believe that there is any such constitutional distinction. I concede that the class of arrests complained of, can be constitutional only when, in cases of Rebellion or Invasion, the public Safety may require them; and I insist that in such cases, they are constitutional *wherever* the public safety does require them—as well in places to which they may prevent the rebellion extending, as in those where it may be already prevailing—as well where they may restrain mischievous interference with the raising and supplying of armies, to suppress the rebellion, as where the rebellion may actually be—as well where they may restrain the enticing men out of the army, as where they would prevent mutiny in the army—equally constitutional at all places where they will conduce to the public Safety, as against the dangers of Rebellion or Invasion.

Take the particular case mentioned by the meeting. They assert in substance that Mr. Vallandigham was by a military commander, seized and tried "for no other reason than words addressed to a public meeting, in criticism of the course of the administration, and in condemnation of the military orders of that general." Now, if there be no mistake about this—if this assertion is the truth and the whole truth—if there was no other reason for the arrest, then I concede that the arrest was wrong. But the arrest, as I understand, was made for a very different reason. Mr. Vallandigham avows his hostility to the war on the part of the Union; and his arrest was made because he was laboring, with some effect, to prevent the raising of troops, to encourage desertions from the army, and to leave the rebellion without an adequate military force to suppress it. He was not arrested because he was damaging the political prospects of the administration, or the personal interests of the commanding general; but because he was damaging the army, upon the existence, and vigor of which, the life of the nation depends. He was warring upon the military; and this gave the military constitutional jurisdiction to lay hands upon him. If Mr. Vallandigham was not damaging the military power of the country, then his arrest was made on mistake of fact, which I would be glad to correct, on reasonably satisfactory evidence.

I understand the meeting, whose resolutions I am considering, to be in favor of suppressing the rebellion by military force—by armies. Long experience has shown that armies can not be maintained unless desertion shall be punished by the severe penalty of death. The case requires, and the law and the constitution, sanction this punishment. Must I shoot a simple-minded soldier boy who deserts, while I must not touch a hair of a wiley agitator who induces him to desert? This is none the less injurious when effected by getting a father, or brother, or friend, into a public meeting, and there working upon his feelings, till he is persuaded to write the soldier boy, that he is fighting in a bad cause, for a wicked administration of a contemptable government, too weak to arrest and punish him if he shall desert. I think that in such a case, to silence the agitator, and save the boy, is not only constitutional, but, withal, a great mercy.

If I be wrong on this question of constitutional power, my error lies in believing that certain proceedings are constitutional when, in cases of rebellion or Invasion, the public Safety requires them, which would not be constitutional when, in absence of rebellion or invasion, the public Safety does not require them—in other words, that the constitution is not in it's application in all respects the same, in cases of Rebellion or invasion, involving the public Safety, as it is in times of profound peace and public security. The constitution itself makes the distinction; and I can no more be persuaded that the government can constitutionally take no strong measure in time of rebellion, because it can be shown that the same could not be lawfully taken in time of peace, than I can be persuaded that a particular drug is not good medicine for a sick man, because it can be shown to not be good food for a well one. Nor am I able to appreciate the danger, apprehended by the meeting, that the American people will, by means of military arrests during the rebellion, lose the right of public discussion, the liberty of speech and the press, the law of evidence, trial by jury, and Habeas corpus, throughout the indefinite peaceful future which I trust lies before them, any more than I am able to believe that a man could contract so strong an appetite for emetics during temporary illness, as to persist in feeding upon them through the remainder of his healthful life.

In giving the resolutions that earnest consideration which you request of me, I can not overlook the fact that the meeting speak as "Democrats." Nor can I, with full respect for their known intelligence, and the fairly presumed deliberation with which they prepared their resolutions, be permitted to suppose that this occurred by accident, or in any way other than that they preferred to designate themselves "democrats" rather than "American citizens." In this time of national peril I would have preferred to meet you upon a level one step higher than any party platform; because I am sure that from such more elevated position, we could do better battle for the country we all love, than we possibly can from those lower ones, where from the force of habit, the prejudices of the past, and selfish hopes of the future, we are sure to expend much of our ingenuity and strength, in finding fault with, and aiming blows at each other. But since you have denied me this, I will yet be thankful, for the country's sake, that not all democrats have done so. He on whose discretionary judgment Mr. Vallandigham was arrested and tried, is a democrat, having no old party affinity with me; and the judge who rejected the constitutional view expressed in these resolutions, by refusing to discharge Mr. V. on Habeas Corpus, is a democrat of better days than these, having received his judicial mantle at the hands of President Jackson. And still more, of all those democrats who are nobly exposing their lives and shedding their blood on the battle-field, I have learned that many approve the course taken with Mr. V. while I have not heard of a single one condemning it. I can not assert that there are none such.

And the name of President Jackson recalls a bit of pertinent history. After the battle of New-Orleans, and while the fact that the treaty of peace had been concluded, was well known in the city, but before official knowledge of it had arrived, Gen. Jackson still maintained martial, or military law. Now, that it could be said the war was over, the clamor against martial law, which had existed from the first, grew more furious. Among other things a Mr. Louiallier published a denunciatory newspaper article. Gen. Jackson arrested him. A lawyer by the name of Morel procured the U.S. Judge Hall to order a writ of Habeas Corpus to release Mr. Louaillier. Gen. Jackson arrested both the lawyer and the judge. A Mr. Hollander ventured to say of some part of the matter that "it was a dirty trick." Gen. Jackson arrested him. When the officer undertook to serve the writ of Habeas Corpus, Gen. Jackson took it from him and sent him away with a copy. Holding the judge in custody a few days, the general sent him beyond the limits of his encampment, and set him at liberty, with an order to remain till the ratification of peace should be regularly announced, or until the British should have left the Southern coast. A day or two more elapsed, the ratification of the treaty of peace was regularly announced, and the judge and others were fully liberated. A few days more, and the judge called Gen. Jackson into court and fined him a thousand dollars, for having arrested him and the others named. The general paid the fine, and there the matter rested for nearly thirty years, when congress refunded principal and interest. The late Senator [Stephen A.] Douglas, then in the House of Representatives, took a leading part in the debate, in which the constitutional question was much discussed. I am not prepared to say whom the Journals would show to have voted for the measure.

It may be remarked: First, that we had the same constitution then, as now. Secondly, that we then had a case of Invasion, and that now we have a case of Rebellion, and: Thirdly, that the permanent right of the people to public discussion, the liberty of speech and the press, the trial by jury, the law of evidence, and the Habeas Corpus, suffered no detriment whatever by that conduct of Gen. Jackson, or it's subsequent approval by the American congress.

And yet, let me say that in my own discretion, I do not know whether I would have ordered the arrest of Mr. V. While I can not shift the responsibility from myself, I hold that, as a general rule, the commander in the field is the better judge of the necessity in any particular case. Of course I must practice a general directory and revisory power in the matter.

One of the resolutions expresses the opinion of the meeting that arbitrary arrests will have the effect to divide and distract those who should be united in suppressing the rebellion; and I am specifically called on to discharge Mr. Vallandigham. I regard this as, at least, a fair appeal to me, on the expediency of exercising a constitutional power which I think exists. In response to such appeal I have to say it gave me pain when I learned that Mr. V. had been arrested,—that is, I was pained that there should have seemed to be a necessity for arresting him – and that it will afford me great pleasure to discharge him so soon as I can, by any means, believe the public safety will not suffer by it. I further say, that as the war progresses, it appears to me, opinion, and action, which were in great confusion at first, take shape, and fall into more regular channels; so that the necessity for arbitrary dealing with them gradually decreases. I have every reason to desire that it would cease altogether; and far from the least is my regard for the opinions and wishes of those who, like the meeting at Albany, declare their purpose to sustain the government in every constitutional and lawful measure to suppress the rebellion. Still, I must continue to do so much as may seem to be required by the public safety.

A. LINCOLN.

ABOUT THE CONTRIBUTORS

Joseph W. Bellacosa, recently retired from the state's highest court, the Court of Appeals, is Dean of the Law School at St. John's University, his alma mater. He has written a number of articles on Lincoln and *habeas corpus*.

Iver Bernstein, Professor of History at Washington University in St. Louis, is the author of *The New York City Draft Riots: Their Significance for American Society and Politics in the Age of the Civil War* (1989).

Laurence M. Hauptman is Professor of History at the State University of New York at New Paltz and is an expert on the history of Native Americans.

Harold Holzer, Vice President for Communications and Marketing at The Metropolitan Museum of Art and co-chair of the U.S. Lincoln Bicentennial Commission, is the author or co-author of nineteen books on Lincoln and the Civil War.

Jeff Shaara is the author of *Gods and Generals* (1996) and *The Last Full Measure* (1998), two best-selling and critically praised novels of the Civil War. His recent *Gone for Soldiers* (2000) explored the Mexican War.

Lonnie R. Speer wrote the definitive study *Portals to Hell: Military Prisons of the Civil War* (1997). A North Carolina-based freelance writer, he has contributed articles to *Civil War Times Illustrated* and *America's Civil War*.

Hans L. Trefousse, Distinguished Professor of History Emeritus at Brooklyn College and the City University of New York Graduate

Center, is the author of acclaimed biographies of Andrew Johnson, Carl Schurz, and Thaddeus Stevens, among other books.

Frank J. Williams, Chief Justice of the Rhode Island Supreme Court, is chairman of the Lincoln Forum, a leading Lincoln collector, and the editor of two books on Lincoln. His collected lectures will be published in 2002.

Lillian S. Williams is Associate Professor of History at the State University of New York at Albany and Director of the school's Institute for Research on Women.

INDEX